Capabilities for Talent Development

Shaping the Future of the Profession

Pat Galagan | Morgean Hirt | Courtney Vital

ATD Press is an internationally renowned source of insightful and practical information on talent development, training, and professional development.

ATD Press
1640 King Street
Alexandria, VA 22314 USA

Ordering information: Books published by ATD Press can be purchased by visiting ATD's website at www.td.org/books or by calling 800.628.2783 or 703.683.8100.

Library of Congress Control Number: 2019953141

ISBN-10: 1-947308-89-0
ISBN-13: 978-1-947308-89-3
e-ISBN: 978-1-950496-51-8

ATD Press Editorial Staff
Director: Sarah Halgas
Manager: Melissa Jones
Community of Practice Manager, Learning & Development: Eliza Blanchard
Developmental Editor: Jack Harlow
Associate Editor: Melissa Jones
Text Design: Shirley E.M. Raybuck
Cover Design: Rose Richey

Printed by P.A. Hutchison Company, Mayfield, PA

Contents

Foreword

ATD has created models of the profession as it evolves for more than 40 years. Based on studies of the forces that influence the field and research about the knowledge, skills, abilities, and behaviors required of its professionals, the successive models have defined and advanced the profession. Taken together, the models reveal the arc of change that has transformed the profession from a tactical focus on training workers to a broader role of developing talent in organizations so they can achieve current goals and prepare for future success.

Those of you who have been in the profession a long time are aware of the increasing value of employee know-how, as well as the ability to apply that knowledge. Organizations are only as agile and successful as their ability to enable learning and change. The capability of their workforce is the differentiator that sets apart successful companies. And as many organizations demonstrate today, their reliance on talent development has moved the function to the senior ranks of leadership.

Those of you who are new to the profession will find that building your own capabilities is critical to success and advancement on your career journey. The new ATD Capability Model, and the research that backs it up, define the personal, professional, and organizational impact capabilities required for success. I encourage you to study and apply the model and use it as a guide for knowledge, skill, and career development in this field.

As we launch the new ATD Capability Model, we owe deep thanks to our research partners at Human Resources Research Organization (HumRRO) who guided ATD staff through all phases of the research, analysis, and model building. We also give special thanks to Elaine Biech, John Coné, and William Rothwell. We're also grateful to the 25 members of the Competency Study Task Force and Advisory Panel, who helped ATD shape the survey and analyze the trends and study findings. (For the full list of project contributors, see page 105.)

Everyone in the profession has an unprecedented opportunity to help individuals and organizations succeed. Thank you for engaging with ATD and for joining the thousands of talent development professionals worldwide who give this field its vitality, and by your performance, its reputation for delivering results. With your help, ATD will continue to empower professionals to develop talent in the workplace. Please let us know how we can continue to help you grow in your career.

—Tony Bingham
  President and CEO
  ATD

Introduction

For more than 75 years, an integral part of ATD's mission has been to establish standards of excellence for our profession through our competency research. We have witnessed continuous evolutions in workplace dynamics and have watched as technology fundamentally altered how we work. Best practices and expectations for the field have kept pace with changing times, and ATD's commitment to equipping others to develop talent in the workplace remains strong. Our industry standard–setting research has helped talent development (TD) professionals—along with managers and leaders who foster talent in organizations—assess, upgrade, and expand their functional skills and connect training and workforce development to organizational strategies and goals. ATD has certified nearly 3,000 TD professionals to date and has trained more than 100,000 learners through our competency-based education offerings.

Capabilities for Talent Development: Shaping the Future of the Profession represents the next milestone in our rich history. It is our ninth study in 41 years and the first to define the concept of talent development, which better reflects the broader functional responsibility and strategic influence of learning professionals. The study provides a comprehensive summary of the research ATD conducted in partnership with the Human Resources Research Organization (HumRRO), a nonprofit research and consulting firm dedicated to supporting quality testing and training programs that improve human, occupational, and organizational effectiveness.

The study lays out the major societal forces and business changes that are requiring professionals to adopt new approaches and upgrade skills to keep pace. It provides a common language to equip a network of global practitioners with shared definitions, methodologies, and concepts. And, it serves as a signal to the profession of what is most critical to know and do in the work of developing others.

What Is Talent Development and What Do TD Professionals Do?

The talent development field is deep and wide. In this book, talent development refers to the efforts that foster learning and employee development to drive organizational performance, productivity, and results.

Talent development includes a rich history of theories and practices, and its practitioners have varied backgrounds and expertise. While many enter the profession through human resource or organization development education and experiences, many others do not. Subject matter experts get tapped to teach others. Many come to talent development after careers in other fields. Regardless of their starting position, talent development professionals are committed to helping others learn and grow, enabling change and transformation.

Research Methodology Overview

The study was conducted throughout 2018 and 2019 with the help of multiple expert groups identified by ATD to play key roles in the process. A 13-member advisory panel of industry experts provided guidance to support the design and implementation of the study, including sharing insights about the profession, identifying emerging trends, recommending literature for review, interpreting results of the occupational survey, and advising ATD on the study methodology.

Aligned to research best practices, the study methodology centers around an occupational survey that was administered to a large, representative sample of TD professionals worldwide. The study's design and development was supported by a 12-member task force. More than 3,000 professionals from 73 countries provided complete responses (23 percent of the participants were located outside the United States). Respondents evaluated the importance of 197 competencies for successful job performance now and in the next three to five years. The data was aggregated and statistical analyses were performed to examine the distribution and magnitude of respondents' ratings. (Appendix C details the data collection process and its findings.)

The advisory panel reviewed the survey results to determine which knowledge and skills are relevant and important for successful performance in talent development. In making the determination, they considered multiple pieces of information, including the competency survey ratings, the number and variety of competencies, and their own experience and knowledge of the profession. Of the 197 competencies included on the survey, the advisory panel identified 188 as important for successful performance as a TD professional now and in the next three to five years.

The foundation of the capability model research entailed capturing the major shifts in society and the larger business landscape since the previous model was published. The major changes in our field were identified through a comprehensive literature review, expert practitioner interviews, and Advisory Panel discussions. These trends spanned a variety of areas in business, technology, learning, science, and the profession itself.

> **THOUGHT LEADER VOICES**
>
> Talent development professionals can't just be experts in learning or instruction design. They have to have a holistic, strategic level of thinking. Companies are really looking for that.
>
> —Nicole Carter, Talent Manager, US Venture Inc.

The most notable finding from the trends research was that talent development no longer simply focuses on the tactical aspects of the design and delivery of learning. Instead, the TD field has become a key element in the success and competitive advantage of organizations, making its practitioners essential partners with all areas of a business in achieving organizational goals.

With most aspects of business on a fast track, talent development professionals are turning to accelerated learning that can be self-directed, individualized, and quickly updated. They are helping learners gain independence and control over what they're learning, which is increasingly available just in time in customized chunks.

TD professionals need critical skills such as business and technology acumen, data analysis, and content curation. They're spending more time partnering with other business units and focusing the attention of learners for maximum efficiency. In an age of artificial intelligence and big data, TD professionals face new challenges in analyzing and interpreting data, deriving insights, and summarizing findings.

With the proliferation of data, TD professionals have new sources and means for capturing the effectiveness of their efforts. Measuring and evaluating the impact of talent development is a must-do to make a meaningful business case for the real value of investing in people. Equally important is the need for practitioners in our field to be strong advisors and partners to the managers and leaders of the businesses they serve.

From Competency to Capability

While past studies have culminated in a competency model framework, ATD's focus has broadened to helping TD professionals build capability that will not only help them be competent performing their work today, but also prepared for challenges they'll face in the future. Competence refers to having the knowledge and skills necessary to perform a job. It remains integral to performance and is one element of capability; however, capability is about adapting and flexing to meet future needs. Competence is about the current state; capability involves the "integration of knowledge, skills, and personal qualities used effectively and appropriately in response to varied, familiar, and unfamiliar circumstances" (Nagarajan and Prabhu 2015).

Influential management thought leader Seth Godin has said "competency is no longer a scarce commodity." The Internet and the ubiquity of information has made it possible to learn about anything, at any time. Simply knowing things is no longer a career advantage. Today's professionals need to put that knowledge to work to create, innovate, lead, manage change, and demonstrate impact. Practitioners need to go beyond the "doing" of designing, developing, and delivering learning solutions to anticipating and diagnosing individual and organizational needs and creating situations that enable individuals to reach their full potential. Regardless of their role or specialty, those who align their work to the bigger picture of how talent creates competitive advantage and supports organizational strategy will deliver the most impact.

> **THOUGHT LEADER VOICES**
>
> The portfolio of a talent development person has expanded—they've got to better leverage and understand the theories and principles of leadership development.
>
> —Robert Brinkerhoff, Professor, Western Michigan University

Overview of the Model

The model answers the question: What should talent development professionals know and do to be successful? Our research generated a body of evidence that supports a valid interpretation of the required knowledge and skills, which became the components of the model. This process begins with the identification of the underlying personal and professional attributes required or expected of TD professionals in relation to their performance at work and ends with the construction of a graphic illustration that depicts the major capability areas needed by individuals in the field.

Because professions are always evolving, models need to be updated periodically to accurately represent changes in the scope and nature of work. For ATD, this has typically been every five to seven years. The current study reflects practice today and five years into the future. However, two important alterations were introduced for the present study.

First, the focus of the analysis was shifted to assess the talent development profession globally. Prior studies focused on training and development and emphasized U.S.-based principles and practices. Broadening the focus to include the entire talent development profession introduced a larger population of individual practitioners performing in a wider array of roles that revealed new competencies to be included in the model.

Second, the unit of analysis was shifted to focus on attributes that are universally applicable (for example, knowledge and skills). A focus on behaviors, attitudes, work activities, or job tasks can be useful, but these attributes tend to be less stable across individuals, organizations, cultures, and regions of the world.

To that end, the new model is structured around three domains of practice:
- capabilities that derive from interpersonal skills
- capabilities that come from building professional knowledge related to developing people and helping them learn
- capabilities that affect an organization's ability to drive toward results and mission success.

In addition, 23 capabilities detailing the core components of the field are included within the three domains.

Applying the Model

The new ATD Capability Model is future-oriented, flexible, and customizable. Above all, it has been designed to be a practical road map for success in the talent development profession. It can be used to assess current skills and expand a practitioner's scope into new functional areas or to align personal training plans. An organization may also use it to determine how to structure and staff a talent development department. Inside this book are application tips for individuals, educators, and organizations, as well as examples and interviews detailing application in the field.

Regardless of how you choose to apply the model, we hope you will take the opportunity to create an action plan for yourself, your clients, and your organization.

A Call to Action

The ability of talent development professionals to pursue new knowledge and expand their skills will be a determining factor for success in the future of work. And given that it is an important responsibility to develop others, we should remember the importance of developing ourselves.

1

What Is Talent Development?

Talent development has almost as many definitions as there are people who practice it. Definitions vary by country and culture, by industry, by organizational strategy, and by the responsibilities of the people practicing it. To some, talent development is an important tool for unleashing human potential. To others, it is a set of practical capabilities for driving organizational performance, productivity, and results. Talent development may also be a primary mechanism for driving organizational performance, productivity, and results by creating the processes, systems, and frameworks that foster learning to maximize individual performance, and for collaborating with business leaders to align development activities with strategic business priorities and outcomes.

Talent development is also a profession—an occupation filled with talented and passionate individuals that involves training and formal qualifications. To support the field, ATD develops models specifying what a TD professional needs to know and be able to do. This is common practice in most professions.

The ATD Certification Institute (ATD CI), an independent organization created by ATD to set industry standards for the talent development profession, administers two credentials based on the ATD models. An associate-level credential is available to those early in their career, with a professional-level credential available to those with more extensive experience.

The Evolution of the Profession

To understand where the profession is headed requires looking back at the history of talent development. First known as training, the field established a foothold in organizations through the design of instruction and its delivery to employees, managers, and leaders to equip them to perform their jobs with success. Training took over where formal education left off, preparing employees to be successful in work roles that were often particular to an industry or organization.

Over the years, as organizations and the work their employees did became more complex and as successful performance came to depend more on employees' know-how and the ability to learn and change, training morphed into a broad set of capabilities focused on improving organizational performance. Training and workplace learning continued its evolution to talent development as focus shifted from providing instruction to enabling employees to learn and grow by the best and most appropriate methods talent developers could make available. Members of the profession stepped up to the role of strategic partner with the responsibility of deliberately enhancing human capability in the service of operational excellence.

Today, the role of many talent development functions is to tie development to the organization, drive the learning agenda, optimize the learning environment, and leverage the technology and science of learning.

> **THOUGHT LEADER VOICES**
>
> As trusted advisors guiding decisions on talent development and change management, trainers become policy makers, consultants, business partners, and even analysts.
> —Jonathan Halls, President and CEO, Jonathan Halls & Associates

Who Are TD Professionals and What Do They Do?

Talent development is a rich tapestry of theories and practices, and its practitioners have always come from a variety of starting points. Some begin as subject matter experts who are tapped to teach others. Some enter the profession with degrees in fields such as human resource development or organizational behavior. Many others come to the profession from careers in fields as diverse as education, economics, engineering, political science, psychology, management, and the humanities.

TD professionals hold education and learning in high esteem, and as a group they are well educated. ATD research in 2019 showed that among U.S.-based TD professionals, 87 percent had at least a four-year college degree, 44 percent had a master's degree, and 5 percent had doctoral or professional degrees. The most common subject areas for a master's degree, besides human resources and organization development, were business, business administration, and education, including instructional design, educational technology, and curriculum and instruction.

In addition, TD professionals play many roles, ranging from specialists such as instructional designers, coaches, or consultants, to generalists who use a broad spectrum of practices to achieve organizational goals. All practitioners have the responsibility to foster learning, use technology to

maximize its accessibility, and partner with others to align development with strategic priorities. These pathways to the talent development field engender different perspectives on the scope of practice. As a result, there is no single type of TD professional.

Today, TD professionals serve in organizations and as consultants and are the leading agents of change and transformation in many organizations. They work to align learning with new directions and help firms manage the human elements of change. It is now common for TD professionals to advance to top-level roles serving the priorities of CEOs and executive teams.

Variety in the talent development profession is also reflected in the changing demographics of ATD members. Founded 75 years ago as the American Society of Training Directors, the association originally served practitioners in the United States. Today, ATD members represent 123 countries spanning six continents. Top countries include Australia, Canada, China, Germany, India, Japan, Korea, Saudi Arabia, Singapore, and the United Kingdom.

Changes in the Work Environment

In the years since the release of the 2013 ASTD Competency Model, the world's work environment has changed considerably. Technology has enabled the disruption of entire industries and forced many organizations to adapt in real time to stay viable. Predicting and developing human capability to meet future goals has become a strategy for success.

Economists, social scientists, neurologists, educators, game developers, tech entrepreneurs, and consultants all have something to say about where work is headed in the future. Many of their predictions are similar: Work will be more collaborative and team-oriented, more automated, and more entangled with social technology. And it will change faster than ever.

However, one thing is already clear: Work in the future will demand more learning and the ability to learn faster.

For the talent development profession, three evergreen topics—leadership, change, and technology—are likely to remain important in the future, but technology will consume greater attention because it will continue to revolutionize the way people buy, work, communicate,

THOUGHT LEADER VOICES

How organizations manage talent is one of the only discernible competitive advantages left as they get bigger and become more automated.
—Karl Kapp, Professor and Consultant, Bloomsburg University, Institute for Interactive Technologies

and learn. IBM CEO Ginni Rometty has said, "Every job will require some technology, and therefore we'll have to revamp education. The K-12 curriculum is obvious, but it's the adult retraining—lifelong learning systems—that will be even more important."

It's a safe assumption that upskilling employees and steering them to new careers will be a larger part of TD professionals' work in the near future. So will efforts to help people work collaboratively using technology. Other new roles might involve mediating the use of social tools for learning and work, helping learners manage their learning time, and increasing organizations' social media savvy. Change management will also be bigger than ever.

It seems certain that artificial intelligence (AI) will be a defining issue in the workplace of the future—and a hard one to keep up with because the technology advances constantly. Many express wariness of AI because it's predicted to take away jobs through automation and will require reskilling for those who are displaced by it. Experts believe that creative jobs and those requiring social interaction, such as managing people, will be safe for a while, but many more types of work will disappear or become too technical for the people who currently hold them. The management consulting firm McKinsey & Company predicts full employment for humans until 2030 but also says that half of today's work activities could be automated using current technology.

Based on this continuous change and uncertainty, ATD's 2019 Competency Study determined that the model for the profession should include, for the first time, specific skills related to imagining and preparing for the future of learning and work.

A Capability Model for You

Success in this new landscape of talent development requires a shift to a proactive, business-partner mindset. Professionals in the future will need to anticipate and diagnose individual and organizational needs and create situations that enable individuals to reach their full potential.

Whether you are a trainer, an independent consultant, or a director of a learning function within an organization, and whether you are entering the field at the beginning of your career or have transitioned to it later in life, you are a TD professional. We have designed the ATD Capability Model for you—to reflect what you need to know and do now and in the future as a TD professional operating on the leading edge of best practice.

2

The ATD
Capability Model

Since 1978, nine competency studies and models have tracked the evolution of the profession from a focus on training design and delivery to its broader role as a strategic business partner. The 1983 Models for Excellence study was the first to define training and development. In 1989, Models for HRD Practice redefined the profession to include career and organization development. The focus of the 1996 model was human performance improvement, followed two years later by the ASTD Models for Learning Technologies, and then Models for Workplace Learning and Performance in 1999. The 2004 model provided a foundation for competency-based certification.

The 2013 Competency Study addressed changes driven by the collapse of the global economy in 2008 and the resulting recession. It was the first to address the impact on the profession of digital, mobile, and social technologies transforming the workplace. And it drew attention to the mindset shift occurring in the workforce with the arrival of new generations of workers. The study also challenged long-held assumptions about talent management, measurement and evaluation of learning's impact, employee engagement, and worker expectations. It treated learning as a process rather than a discrete event and found that facilitating and enabling learning environments was overtaking training delivery as a primary role in the profession.

Three of the factors that influenced the 2013 Competency Model have intensified in the following five years: rapidly advancing technologies, demographic shifts in the workforce, and the pace of globalization. Today's newest generations of workers expect to be offered opportunities to learn and grow. They bring a culture of connectivity and social networking to their jobs. They value learning couched in experiences and are fluid learners, although some are inexperienced in selecting and evaluating learning content.

These forces are reshaping jobs, industries, and organizations, as well as the practice of talent development. They also influenced the design of ATD's 2019 Capability Model.

The Model

The 2019 study found that the knowledge, skills, and abilities (KSAs) of effective TD professionals at all levels of their career fell into three major domains of practice: capabilities that derive from interpersonal skills, capabilities that come from building professional knowledge related to developing people and helping them learn, and capabilities that impact an entire organization's ability to drive toward results and mission success. Within those three broad domains of practice, the KSAs are grouped into 23 capabilities.

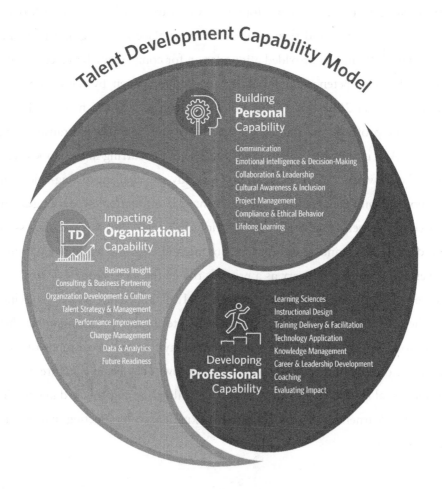

Key findings in the 2019 research included the need for TD professionals at all levels to view the entire talent development ecosystem holistically. While a TD professional may have a specific area of focus as an instructional designer or a coach, they need to understand how their work fits into and affects the larger organization. By blending capabilities across the three domains, TD professionals will become as capable and effective as possible. To that end, there is no hierarchy in the new capability model—each of the three major domains of practice hold key elements to success.

Unlike the previous model, which outlined 10 areas of expertise, the new model is not intended to have one specific capability stand alone for a job role. For example, the training delivery and facilitation capability does not contain everything that someone whose primary role is to lead training sessions will need to know and be able to do. Rather, the knowledge and skill represented in that capability plus knowledge and skill across other capabilities that run across several other areas of the model will make them most able to successfully perform in their role.

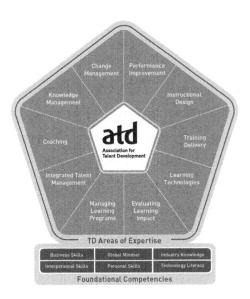

Likewise, for every hundred talent developmental professionals, there will be a hundred different job descriptions, and just as many variances in the responsibilities of their roles. For that reason, the new model is designed to be customized to an individual's roles and responsibilities. Grouping the necessary knowledge and skills into more discrete capabilities allows individuals, talent development functions, and organizations to take those knowledge and skills most applicable to them and focus on their development.

From Competency to Capability

Several groups and stakeholders, including the advisory group and the leadership of ATD's Chief Talent Development Officers network, provided input into the next iteration of the model. Discussions regarding "competency" revealed concerns that the term was limiting and outdated. Further discussions led to a consensus that "capability" should replace "competency" as the model's descriptor.

Competency is a concept identified 60 years ago by organizational psychologist R.W. White through his work exploring theories of motivation. In human resource parlance, competence is defined as "the set of demonstrable characteristics and skills that enable and improve the efficiency and performance of a job."

Capability, by contrast, refers broadly to ability and the quality or state of being capable. The *Business Dictionary* defines capability as "a measure of the ability of an entity (department, organization, person, system) to achieve its objectives, especially in relation to its overall mission."

The 2019 ATD model departs from the term "competency" and uses the broader notion of capability as the capacity to achieve objectives, whether personal or organizational. It implies action and impact. "Capability," according the *Merriam Webster Dictionary,* also refers to "a feature or faculty capable of development," in other words, to potentiality. This is consistent with the perspective of talent development as a tool for unleashing human potential.

This change is expressed in the new model by grouping the domains of talent development into those that are for developing personal capability, building professional capability, and impacting organizational capability required for professional success.

Future-Oriented and Customizable

Those familiar with previous ATD competency models will notice changes in the 2019 model that make it better suited to the complexities of the talent development profession today.

The new model is future-oriented, reflecting the field of talent development now but also five years in the future. It responds to these trends affecting talent development, such as digital transformation, data analytics, information availability, and partnerships between talent development and the business. It also anticipates a future workplace transformed by artificial intelligence and a workforce composed of a majority of part-time and contract workers.

The new model is flexible and updatable. In the 41 years that ATD has been developing and updating its models, the "what" of the profession has changed gradually. However, especially in recent years, the "how" has changed rapidly as focus shifts from tactics for imparting knowledge to broad concepts for enabling learning and partnering with the business. The KSAs detailed in the 23 capabilities of the 2019 model are broader and less context-specific than in the past and thus are easier to update.

The advisors to the study also noted the increasing fluidity of roles in talent development due to the size of the organization, the amount of technology in use, and surrounding issues such as industry disruption and decline, or conversely, a rapid rise in size and influence. The industry has entered a time in which a job no longer equals a single role and work is often defined by projects and done in teams; thus, the advisors recommended that the model be interactive and customizable. Today, TD practitioners' roles range from instructors to catalysts for growth and innovation, leaders of change, enablers of learning, developers of workplace capability, and business partners.

> **THOUGHT LEADER VOICES**
>
> Talent development needs to enhance the organization's ability to learn quickly because that's now the basis for competition.
>
> —John Coné, Principal, The Eleventh Hour Group

The Model Domains and Capabilities

The 2019 ATD Capability Model includes three major domains or areas of skill required, under which are 23 capability areas. The model depicts the major domains as adjoining units to indicate there is no hierarchy implied.

- Developing Personal Capability
  - › Communication
  - › Emotional Intelligence & Decision Making
  - › Collaboration & Leadership

- › Cultural Awareness & Inclusion
- › Project Management
- › Compliance & Ethical Behavior
- › Lifelong Learning
- Building Professional Capability
  - › Learning Sciences
  - › Instructional Design
  - › Training Delivery & Facilitation
  - › Technology Application
  - › Knowledge Management
  - › Career & Leadership Development
  - › Coaching
  - › Evaluating Impact
- Impacting Organizational Capability
  - › Business Insight
  - › Consulting & Business Partnering
  - › Organization Development & Culture
  - › Talent Strategy & Management
  - › Performance Improvement
  - › Change Management
  - › Data & Analytics
  - › Future Readiness

> **THOUGHT LEADER VOICES**
>
> I think we need to ratchet up our role to become advisors to leaders. Our leaders have so many things on their minds. We need to know what their problems are and how we can help them solve those.
> —Elaine Biech, President, ebb associates inc.

Chapter 4 defines the 23 capabilities, with their specific key knowledge areas and skill areas.

The Occupational Survey Results

The trends identified in the thought leader interviews and reflected in the development of the KSA statements bore themselves out further in the study results. Based on the rating responses to the various knowledge and skill statements, it was clear that front-line TD professionals agree that the role of talent development is critical to organizational success and can be used to drive results and marketplace advantage. (For more information on the occupational survey, see Appendix C.)

The knowledge and skill statements related to interpersonal skills, often called "foundational" or "enabling" competencies, were rated highest in importance as a group under Building Personal Capability (Table 2-1).

Table 2-1. Survey Results for the 23 Capabilities

Domain/Capability	Average Importance Currently	Average Importance in the Future (3-5 years)
Building Personal Capability	3.15	3.34
Communication	3.42	3.56
Emotional Intelligence & Decision Making	3.20	3.36
Collaboration & Leadership	3.06	3.29
Cultural Awareness & Inclusion	3.01	3.27
Project Management	3.07	3.25
Compliance & Ethical Behavior	2.95	3.12
Lifelong Learning	3.37	3.52
Developing Professional Capability	2.94	3.19
Learning Sciences	3.05	3.15
Instructional Design	3.18	3.37
Training Delivery & Facilitation	3.25	3.36
Technology Application	2.81	3.14
Knowledge Management	2.96	3.26
Career & Leadership Development	2.69	3.02
Coaching	2.80	3.13
Evaluating Impact	2.75	3.07
Impacting Organizational Capability	2.94	3.23
Business Insight	2.85	3.24
Consulting & Business Partnering	3.14	3.35
Organization Development & Culture	2.93	3.18
Talent Strategy & Management	2.95	3.25
Change Management	2.89	3.21
Performance Improvement	3.09	3.36
Data & Analytics	2.70	3.04
Future Readiness	3.00	3.27

Note: Each knowledge and skill statement within the capability was rated on a scale of 1-4, where 1 = not important, 2 = minimally important, 3 = moderately important, and 4 = very important.

Overwhelmingly, respondents rated the importance of tasks related to business partnering and those that affect organizational strategy and success equally to, and in some cases higher than, those traditionally viewed as necessary in the training development and delivery field.

This further demonstrates the importance of having capabilities outside the more traditional training and development skill set in order to work effectively. The near equal importance ratings across the three domains highlights the requirements of a blended skill set for TD professionals.

The capabilities with the highest rating of importance further highlight the trends uncovered in interviews with thought leaders and experts—notably, the increasing importance of consulting, partnering, and collaborating, as well as preparing for the rapid changes coming in the future (Table 2-2).

Table 2-2. Capabilities With the Highest Rating of Importance

Domain/Capability	Average Importance Currently	Average Importance in the Future (3-5 years)
Communication	3.42	3.56
Lifelong Learning	3.37	3.52
Instructional Design	3.18	3.37
Training Delivery & Facilitation	3.25	3.36
Emotional Intelligence & Decision Making	3.20	3.36
Consulting & Business Partnering	3.14	3.35
Collaboration & Leadership	3.06	3.29
Future Readiness	3.00	3.27

Note: Each knowledge and skill statement within the capability was rated on a scale of 1-4, where 1 = not important, 2 = minimally important, 3 = moderately important, and 4 = very important.

The Value of the Model

ATD's 2019 Capability Model is designed to show what TD professionals need to know to be successful in their jobs in the current global work environment as well as the near future. It also shows how talent development is a primary mechanism for driving performance, productivity, and operational excellence.

Beyond illustrating the expanding role of talent development, the model has many other applications. Individuals may use it to assess their current knowledge and skills against what they will need to succeed in the future. Or they may use it to determine possible career paths. Further, organizations may use it to see how to staff a talent development function and position that function within the organizational structure. Organizational leaders may use the model to determine the qualifications for a TD executive on a leadership team, or to identify gaps in the capabilities of a TD function. Educators, recruiters, and others could use it to help communicate the scope of the profession to those exploring careers in talent development or planning their professional development. The model is also a valuable resource for those considering ATD's certification offerings. Chapter 4 dives deeper into the possible applications of the model.

> **THOUGHT LEADER VOICES**
>
> We need to get better at finding the intersection between an individual's capabilities and the emerging needs of the organization.
>
> —John Coné, Principal, The Eleventh Hour Group

Before moving on to application, we'll first explore further the domains and capabilities that make up the model.

3

The ATD Model Domains and Capabilities

As noted in previous chapters, the new ATD Capability Model is significantly different than previous competency models for the field. In this chapter you will see the broad domains of practice, the related capabilities, and the knowledge and skills associated with each capability.

Developing Personal Capability

This domain of practice embodies the foundational or "enabling" abilities all working professionals should possess to be effective in the business world. These largely interpersonal skills, often called "soft skills," are needed to build effective organizational or team culture, trust, and engagement.

Communication

Communication is about connecting with others. Effectively communicating requires a knowledge of communication principles and techniques that allows a person to articulate the appropriate message for a particular audience. It requires active listening, facilitating dialogue, and the ability to express thoughts, feelings, and ideas clearly, concisely, and compellingly.

Key Knowledge Areas

Research results returned only capability statements for this capability.

Key Capabilities

An effective TD professional will need skill in:

- expressing thoughts, feelings, and ideas in a clear, concise, and compelling manner

- applying principles of active listening (for example, focusing on what someone is saying, deferring judgment, and responding appropriately)
- using communication strategies that inform and influence audiences
- applying persuasion and influencing techniques to gain agreement, commitment, and buy-in from stakeholders
- conceiving, developing, and delivering information in various formats and media (for example reports, briefings, memorandums, presentations, articles, and emails)
- applying verbal, written, and nonverbal communication techniques (for example, agenda setting, asking open-ended questions, use of posture and deference, and demonstrating professional presence)
- facilitating dialogue with individuals and groups to help them identify, articulate, and clarify their thoughts and feelings
- articulating and conveying value propositions to gain agreement, support, and buy-in from stakeholders.

Emotional Intelligence & Decision Making

Emotional intelligence and the ability to make good decisions are paramount to professional success. Emotional intelligence is the ability to understand, assess, and regulate your own emotions; correctly interpret the verbal and nonverbal behaviors of others; and adjust your behavior in relation to others. Emotional intelligence is a key strength in building rapport. Decision making requires one to determine the need and importance of making a decision, identify choices, gather information about choices, and take action on the appropriate choice.

Key Knowledge Areas

A TD professional with capability in this area will need knowledge of:
- theories of emotional intelligence
- techniques and approaches to learn and demonstrate resilience (for example, meditation, mindfulness, and perspective-taking)
- decision-making models (for example, consensus-based, democratic, and autocratic).

Key Capabilities

An effective TD professional will need skill in:

- assessing and managing one's own emotional state
- identifying personal biases that influence one's own cognition and behavior
- observing and interpreting the verbal and nonverbal behavior of individuals and groups
- adjusting their own behavior in response to or anticipation of changes in others' behavior, attitudes, and thoughts
- using logic and reasoning to identify the strengths and weaknesses of alternative solutions, conclusions, or approaches to problems.

Collaboration and Leadership

Leadership is about influence and vision, which also helps facilitate collaboration. Being good at collaboration requires the ability to foster environments that encourage teamwork and respectful relationships, especially cross-functionally. Both collaboration and leadership require the practitioner to communicate effectively, provide feedback, and assess the work of others. Leadership also requires the ability to effectively align people and tasks to support the organization's strategy. Effective leaders inspire trust and engagement with their employees and teams.

> **THOUGHT LEADER VOICES**
>
> Talent development focuses on aligning learning and development activities with the most pressing goals and initiatives of the organization.
> —Catherine Lombardozzi, Founder, Learning 4 Learning Professionals

Key Knowledge Areas

A TD professional with capability in this area will need knowledge of:

- theories, methods, and techniques to build and manage professional relationships (for example, group dynamics, teamwork, shared experience, and negotiation)
- methods and criteria for establishing and managing collaboration among various units (for example, finance, operations, IT, and sales and marketing)
- conflict management techniques

- methods and techniques for managing and supervising others (for example, directing others' work, delegating tasks, providing guidance and support, and allocating tools and resources)
- principles and techniques for providing feedback
- leadership theories (for example, transformational, inclusive, and situational).

Key Capabilities

An effective TD professional will need skill in:

- building and managing teams and work groups (for example, leveraging group dynamics and fostering teamwork and collaboration)
- integrating and synthesizing others' viewpoints to build alignment of diverse perspectives
- managing conflict (for example, providing feedback and mediating and resolving disputes)
- matching, assigning, and delegating work to others.

Cultural Awareness & Inclusion

Cultural awareness and the ability to foster an inclusive work environment are requirements in today's global business climate. Being effective at both means conveying respect for different perspectives, backgrounds, customs, abilities, and behavior norms, as well as ensuring all employees are respected and involved by leveraging their capabilities, insights, and ideas.

Key Knowledge Areas

A TD professional with capability in this area will need knowledge of:

- cultural differences in the workplace (for example, styles of communication, organizational and business customs, attire, and family obligations)
- social and cultural norms that influence decision making and behavior
- methods and techniques to foster cultural awareness, encourage cultural sensitivity, and broaden viewpoints
- approaches to encourage and promote workplace diversity and inclusion.

Key Capabilities

An effective TD professional will need skill in:

- adapting and adjusting attitude, perspective, and behavior to function effectively in diverse environments or situations
- integrating diversity and inclusion principles in talent development strategies and initiatives.

Project Management

Analyzing and prioritizing elements of a learning initiative or talent solution helps to ensure a meaningful and relevant learner experience. Effective project management requires being able to plan, organize, direct, and control resources for a finite period to complete specific goals and objectives.

Key Knowledge Areas

A TD professional with capability in this area will need knowledge of project management principles and processes (for example, scheduling, planning, allocating resources, evaluating, and reporting).

Key Capabilities

An effective TD professional will need skill in:

- coordinating the logistical tasks associated with planning meetings
- evaluating and prioritizing implications, risks, feasibility, and consequences of potential activities
- developing project plans and schedules that integrate resources, tasks, and timelines
- adjusting work processes and outputs in response to or anticipation of changes in goals, standards, resources, and time
- establishing, monitoring, and communicating progress toward the achievement of goals, objectives, and milestones.

Compliance & Ethical Behavior

Compliance and ethical behavior refer to the expectation that a TD professional acts with integrity and operates within the laws that govern where they work and live. For TD professionals it may also require knowledge of and abiding by the regulations and laws related to content creation, accessibility, human resources, employment, and public policies.

Key Knowledge Areas

A TD professional with capability in this area will need knowledge of:

- laws, regulations, and ethical issues related to the access and use of information (for example, intellectual capital, personally identifiable information, and customer data)
- laws, regulations, and ethical issues related to the development of instructional content (for example, intellectual property and copyright laws and accessibility requirements)
- laws, regulations, and ethical issues related to human resources and talent development (for example, employment law, accessibility, and labor relations)
- laws, regulations, and ethical issues related to the employment of permanent, contingent, and dispersed workforces
- region- or market-specific education and labor public policies.

Key Capabilities

An effective TD professional will need skill in:

- acting with integrity (for example, being honest, acknowledging own mistakes, and treating people with dignity, respect, and fairness)
- establishing, maintaining, and enforcing standards for integrity and ethical behavior in self and others.

Lifelong Learning

Lifelong learning is sometimes called continuous learning, agile learning, or learning drive. It is marked by traits such as self-motivation, insatiable curiosity, and intelligent risk-taking. TD professionals should model the value of lifelong learning by pursuing knowledge for personal and professional reasons. Taking ownership for one's own professional development signals to others that they can and should do the same.

Key Knowledge Areas

A TD professional with capability in this area will need knowledge of:

- how a desire to learn can lead to the expansion and development of knowledge and skills over time
- resources for career exploration and lifelong learning for self and others.

Key Capabilities

An effective TD professional will need skill in:

- acquiring new knowledge through professional development activities for one's self (for example, attending professional conferences, self-directed reading, and monitoring industry trends)
- developing, maintaining, and leveraging networks across a range of people and groups inside and outside the organization (for example, influential people and learning and performance experts).

Building Professional Capability

This domain of practice embodies the knowledge and skills TD professionals should possess to be effective in their roles of creating the processes, systems, and frameworks that foster learning, maximize individual performance, and develop the capacity and potential of employees.

Learning Sciences

Organizations with highly effective learning programs incorporate key principles from the learning sciences, the interdisciplinary, research-based field that works to further the understanding of learning, learning innovation, and instructional methodologies. TD professionals who are applying best practice will understand and apply foundational learning theories, principles of adult learning theory, and cognitive science to design, develop, and deliver solutions that maximize outcomes.

Key Knowledge Areas

A TD professional with capability in this area will need knowledge of:

- the foundational learning theories of behaviorism, cognitivism, and constructivism
- the principles and applications of cognitive science for learning (for example auditory and visual processing, information storage and retrieval, memory, and cognitive load)
- adult learning theories and models (for example, Knowles' Adult Learning Theory, Bloom's Taxonomy, Gagne's Nine Levels of Learning, Mager's Criterion-Referenced Instruction Approach, social and collaborative learning, and experiential learning)
- communication theories and models and how they relate to learning.

Key Capabilities

An effective TD professional will need skill in applying principles of cognitive science and adult learning to design solutions that maximize learning and behavioral outcomes (for example, enhancing motivation and increasing knowledge retention).

Instructional Design

Instructional design is an essential element of an effective learning effort. The creation of learning experiences and materials is what results in the acquisition and application of knowledge and skills. TD professionals follow a system of assessing needs, designing a process, developing materials, and evaluating effectiveness. Instructional design requires the analysis and selection of the most appropriate strategies, methodologies, and technologies to maximize the learning experience and knowledge transfer.

Key Knowledge Areas

A TD professional with capability in this area will need knowledge of:

- instructional design models and processes (for example, ADDIE and SAM)
- needs assessment approaches and techniques

- instructional modalities (for example, classroom learning, blended learning, massive open online courses or MOOCs, gamification, multi-device and mobile learning, and virtual reality simulations)
- methods and techniques for defining learning and behavioral outcome statements
- the criteria used to assess the quality and relevance of instructional content in relation to a desired learning or behavioral outcome
- methods and techniques for planning, designing, and developing instructional content
- types and applications of instructional methods and techniques (for example, discussion, self-directed learning, role playing, lecture, action learning, demonstration, and exercise)
- how design thinking and rapid prototyping can be applied to the development of learning and talent development solutions
- how formal and informal learning experiences influence or support individual and group development.

> **THOUGHT LEADER VOICES**
>
> Thinking in the field has shifted. Now we have the end in mind—what is the organization trying to achieve and how do we work backward from there?
> —Jennifer Martineau, SVP Research, Evaluation & Societal Advancement, Center for Creative Leadership

Key Capabilities

An effective TD professional will need skill in:

- developing learning and behavioral outcome statements
- designing blueprints, schematics, and other visual representations of learning and development solutions (for example, wireframes, storyboards, and mock-ups)
- eliciting and using knowledge and information from subject matter experts to support and enhance learning
- selecting and aligning delivery options and media for training and learning events to the desired learning or behavioral outcomes
- designing and developing learning assets (for example, role plays, self-assessments, training manuals, job aids, and visual aids) that align to a desired learning or behavioral outcome.

Training Delivery & Facilitation

Training delivery and facilitation are means by which TD professionals help individuals improve performance at work by learning new skills and knowledge. The practitioner serves as a catalyst for learning by understanding the learner's needs, creating the right environment for learning, building rapport with participants, and using the appropriate delivery options and media to make learning engaging, effective, relevant, and applicable.

Key Knowledge Areas

A TD professional with capability in this area will need knowledge of facilitation methods and techniques.

Key Capabilities

An effective TD professional will need skill in:

- coordinating the logistical tasks associated with planning meetings and learning events
- facilitating meetings or learning events in face-to-face or virtual environments
- creating positive learning climates and environments
- selecting and aligning delivery options and media for training and learning events to the desired learning or behavioral outcomes
- delivering training using multiple delivery options and media (for example, mobile or multi-device, online, classroom, or multimedia)
- designing and developing learning assets (for example, role plays, self-assessments, training manuals, job aids, and visual aids) that align to a desired learning or behavioral outcome.

Technology Application

Disruption via technology will continue to be a reality for organizations and talent development functions. TD professionals must have the ability to identify, select, and implement the right learning and talent technologies that serve the best interests of the organization and its people. Practitioners should be able to identify opportunities to adapt and leverage the right technologies at the right time to meet organizational goals.

Key Knowledge Areas

A TD professional with capability in this area will need knowledge of:

- criteria and techniques for evaluating and selecting e-learning software and tools
- methods and techniques for testing the usability and functionality of learning technologies and support systems
- existing learning technologies and support systems (for example, collaborative learning software, learning management systems, authoring tools, and social media)
- human resources systems and technology platforms and how they integrate with other organizational and business systems and processes
- communication technologies and their applications (for example, video conferencing, web conferencing, audience response systems, and presentation software)
- principles of user interface design
- functions, features, limitations, and practical applications of the technologies available to support learning and talent development solutions
- techniques and approaches to leverage social media platforms and tools to support knowledge sharing, idea exchange, and learning
- artificial intelligence, machine learning algorithms, augmented reality, and mixed reality that are ethical and free of bias.

Key Capabilities

An effective TD professional will need skill in:

- selecting, integrating, managing, and maintaining learning platforms (for example, learning management systems, knowledge management systems, and performance management systems)
- identifying, defining, and articulating technology system requirements to support learning and talent development solutions

- identifying, selecting, and implementing learning technologies (for example, using evaluative criteria and identifying appropriate applications in an instructional environment)
- developing artificial intelligence, machine learning algorithms, augmented reality, and mixed reality that are ethical and free of bias
- using e-learning software and tools
- using human resource technology systems to store, retrieve, and process talent and talent development–related information.

Knowledge Management

In a knowledge economy, lost institutional knowledge can cost organizations real money in the form of turnover, recruitment, and training costs. Knowledge management is the explicit and systematic management of intellectual capital and organizational knowledge, as well as the associated processes of creating, gathering, validating, categorizing, archiving, disseminating, leveraging, and using intellectual capital for improving the organization and the individuals in it.

Key Knowledge Areas

A TD professional with capability in this area will need knowledge of:
- principles of knowledge management (for example, conceptualizing, managing, preserving, or maintaining organizational knowledge)
- methods and techniques for capturing and codifying knowledge (for example, storytelling, data mining, cognitive mapping, decision trees, or knowledge taxonomies)
- methods and techniques for disseminating or sharing knowledge across individuals, groups, and organizations.

Key Capabilities

An effective TD professional will need skill in:
- designing and implementing knowledge management strategy

- identifying the quality, authenticity, accuracy, impartiality, or relevance of information from various sources (for example, databases, print and online media, speeches and presentations, and observations)
- organizing and synthesizing information from multiple sources (for example, databases, print and online media, speeches and presentations, and observations)
- curating instructional content, tools, and resources (for example, researching, evaluating, selecting, or assembling publicly available online courseware)
- identifying the type and amount of information needed to support talent development activities
- developing, managing, facilitating, or supporting knowledge networks and communities of practice.

Career & Leadership Development

Creating a culture of career development in an organization can be a competitive advantage. Being effective at career and leadership development requires the ability to create planned processes of interaction between the organization and the individual that allow an employee to grow within the organization. Understanding the specific skills and capabilities an organization needs now and in the future is important when developing assessments, programs, and pathways to advance employees within the organization.

Key Knowledge Areas

A TD professional with capability in this area will need knowledge of:
- how to develop and implement qualification programs
- career development methods and techniques (for example, job rotations and stretch assignments)
- career models and paths (such as vertical, horizontal, project-based, and matrix)
- leadership development practices and techniques (for example, formal training programs, job rotation, and coaching or mentoring).

Key Capabilities

An effective TD professional will need skill in:

- developing, administering, and debriefing the results of assessments of intelligence, aptitude, potential, skill, ability, or interests
- facilitating the career development planning process (for example, helping employees identify needs and career goals and preparing development plans)
- conducting individual and group career planning sessions to provide guidance across career phases (for example, onboarding and job changes)
- sourcing, designing, building, and evaluating leadership development experiences.

Coaching

Coaching is a discipline and practice that is an essential capability for any TD professional, and it has the power to catalyze breakthroughs to enhance individual, team, and organizational performance. Coaching is an interactive process that helps individuals develop more rapidly toward a preferred future state, produce results, set goals, take action, make better decisions, and capitalize on their natural strengths. Coaching requires using global listening, asking powerful questions, strengthening conversations, and creating action plans.

Key Knowledge Areas

A TD professional with capability in this area will need knowledge of:

- organizational coaching methods
- methods and techniques to evaluate the effectiveness of coaching
- professional standards and ethical guidelines for coaching.

Key Capabilities

An effective TD professional will need skill in:

- helping individuals or teams identify goals, develop realistic action plans, seek development opportunities, and monitor progress and accountability

- coaching supervisors and managers on methods and approaches for supporting employee development
- creating effective coaching agreements
- establishing an environment that fosters mutual respect and trust with coaching clients
- recruiting, training, and pairing coaches or mentors with employees.

Evaluating Impact

Evaluating the impact of talent development programs is correlated with learning and business effectiveness. TD professionals should be able to implement a multilevel, systematic method for gathering, analyzing, and reporting on information about the effectiveness and effort of learning programs. Collecting data relevant to business strategies and goals helps decision making, improves learning programs, and increases the value proposition of learning with senior leaders and business stakeholders.

Key Knowledge Areas

A TD professional with capability in this area will need knowledge of:
- models and methods to evaluate the impact of learning and talent development solutions
- qualitative and quantitative data collection methods, techniques, and tools (for example, observations, interviews, focus groups, surveys, or assessments)
- research design methodologies and types (for example, experimental, correlational, descriptive, meta-analytic, longitudinal, and cross-sectional).

Key Capabilities

An effective TD professional will need skill in:
- creating data collection tools (for example, questionnaires, surveys, and structured interviews)
- selecting or designing organizational research (for example, defining research questions, creating hypotheses, and selecting methodologies)
- identifying and defining individual or organizational outcome metrics based on the evaluation strategy or business objectives of a solution.

Impacting Organizational Capability

This domain of practice embodies the knowledge, skills, and abilities needed by professionals to ensure talent development is a primary mechanism driving organizational performance, productivity, and results.

Business Insight

To add the most value to an organization, TD professionals should understand business principles and the specific business or organization in which they work. Business insight is the understanding of key factors affecting a business, such as its current situation, influences from its industry or market, and factors influencing growth. It also includes understanding how an organization accomplishes its mission or purpose, makes and spends money, and makes decisions, as well as the internal processes and structures of how work gets done. Having business insight is essential to strategic involvement with top management and ensuring talent development strategies align with overall business strategy.

Key Knowledge Areas

A TD professional with capability in this area will need knowledge of:

- business or organizational processes, operations, and outputs (for example, governance structures, business models, products, and services)

> **THOUGHT LEADER VOICES**
>
> A true TD practitioner asks the business question before jumping to solutions, and thinks critically and analytically when building the case for moving in a direction.
> —Patti Phillips, CEO, ROI Institute

- business strategies and factors that influence an organization's competitive position in the industry
- how organizations provide customer service (for example, anticipating and assessing needs, meeting quality standards for services, and evaluating customer satisfaction)
- how talent development contributes to an organization's competitive advantage
- financial management principles (for example, pricing, contracts, budgeting, accounting, forecasting, and reporting).

Key Capabilities

An effective TD professional will need skill in:

- managing budgets and resources
- creating business cases for talent development initiatives using economic, financial, and organizational data
- communicating business and financial information to different audiences using the appropriate terminology and relevant examples.

Consulting & Business Partnering

Being seen as a valued business partner should be a goal for TD professionals. Consulting and business partnering use expertise, influence, and personal skill to build a two-way relationship that facilitates change or improvement in the business. Clients may be internal or external. Successful consulting and business partnering requires skill in needs assessment, data analysis, communications, systems thinking, problem solving, negotiation, facilitation, and coaching.

Key Knowledge Areas

A TD professional with capability in this area will need knowledge of:

- needs assessment approaches and techniques
- methods and criteria for sourcing, establishing, or managing partnerships (for example, vendors, clients, suppliers, universities, and membership associations).

Key Capabilities

An effective TD professional will need skill in:

- establishing and managing organizational or business partnerships and relationships
- partnering with other organizational units to provide guidance on departmental or organizational talent requirements
- managing stakeholders on an ongoing basis to sustain organizational or business relationships

- synthesizing information to formulate recommendations or a course of
  action to gain agreement, support, or buy-in from stakeholders
- conveying recommendations or a course of action to gain agreement,
  support, or buy-in from stakeholders
- identifying, minimizing, and overcoming organizational barriers to
  implementing talent development solutions or strategies.

Organization Development & Culture

To remain relevant, organizations must continually develop capability and capacity.
Organization development (OD) is an effort that focuses on improving an organization's capability through alignment of strategy, structure, management processes,
people, rewards, and metrics. Organizational culture encompasses the values and
behaviors that contribute to the social and psychological environment of a business.
Understanding an organization's culture, its norms, formal and informal relationships,
power dynamics, and hierarchies informs the planning of initiatives to develop systems, structures, and processes to improve effectiveness.

Key Knowledge Areas

A TD professional with capability in this area will need knowledge of:
- organization development concepts (for example, organizational design, job
  design, team formation, cultural norms, and culture transformation)
- the theories and frameworks related to the design, interaction, and operation
  of social, organizational, and informational systems (for example, systems
  thinking, open systems theory, chaos and complexity theory, network theory,
  and action research)
- the principles of organizational management (for example, division of labor,
  authority and responsibility, equity, order, and unity)
- work roles, relationships, and reporting structures within an organization
- how employee engagement and retention influence organizational outcomes
- the principles, policies, and practices associated with programs and initiatives
  designed for organizational well-being (such as silos, job environment,
  toxicity, goal setting, job stability, and autonomy)

- strategies and techniques for building, supporting, or promoting an organizational culture that values talent and learning as drivers of competitive advantage.

Key Capabilities

An effective TD professional will need skill in:
- designing and implementing organization development strategy
- identifying formal and informal relationships, hierarchies, and power dynamics in an organization
- creating a culture which encourages and creates opportunities for dialogue and feedback between individuals and groups (for example, designing collaborative work practices and spaces, and role-modeling effective feedback techniques)
- assessing and evaluating employee engagement
- designing and implementing employee engagement strategy
- articulating and codifying talent and leadership principles, values, and competencies that guide the organization's culture and define behavioral expectations.

Talent Strategy & Management

For an organization to realize its potential, talent development should be integrated into all components of talent strategy and management. Talent strategy and management are the practices used to build an organization's culture, engagement, capability, and capacity through the implementation and integration of talent acquisition, employee development, retention, and deployment processes, ensuring these processes are aligned to organizational goals. Depending on organizational context and structure, broad partnerships with HR and line leaders will be needed.

Key Knowledge Areas

A TD professional with capability in this area will need knowledge of:
- talent management functions (for example, workforce planning, acquisition, employee development, performance management, and compensation and rewards)

- succession planning and talent review processes (for example, assessment, scenario planning, talent mobility, and critical roles identification)
- methods to identify the critical requirements of tasks, jobs, and roles (for example, job analysis, competency modeling, and leadership competency development)
- talent acquisition strategies and concepts (for example, talent mobility, employment branding, sourcing, passive and active recruiting, and onboarding)
- approaches for identifying and developing high potential talent.

Key Capabilities

An effective TD professional will need skill in:

- creating and aligning the talent development vision and strategy with the organizational and business vision and strategy
- developing a talent strategy that aligns to the organizational strategy to influence organizational outcomes in a positive direction
- designing and implementing strategic plans for talent development projects, programs, or functions
- identifying anticipated constraints or problems affecting talent development initiatives (for example, resource deficiencies or lack of support)
- establishing and executing a marketing strategy to promote talent development
- designing and implementing communication strategy in order to drive talent management objectives
- communicating how talent development strategies and solutions support the achievement of targeted business and organizational results
- communicating the value of learning and professional development
- comparing and evaluating the advantages and disadvantages of talent development strategies (for example, developing internal employees versus hiring external talent)
- developing workforce plans that articulate current and future talent and skill requirements
- designing and implementing a performance management strategy.

Performance Improvement

Organizational competitiveness is fueled by improvement in human performance. Performance improvement is a holistic and systematic approach to meeting organizational goals by identifying and closing human performance gaps. This is a results-based effort that includes the ability to analyze root causes of performance issues, plan for future improvements in human performance, and design and develop solutions to close performance gaps.

Key Knowledge Areas

A TD professional with capability in this area will need knowledge of:
- the theories, models, and principles of human performance improvement
- performance analysis methods and techniques (for example, business process analysis, performance gap assessment, and root-cause analysis)
- how human interactions with work environments, tools, equipment, and technology affect individual and organizational performance.

Key Capabilities

An effective TD professional will need skill in:
- conducting a performance analysis to identify goals, gaps, or opportunities
- designing and developing performance improvement solutions to address performance gaps
- designing and implementing performance support systems and tools (for example, instructional resources, data, process models, job aids, and expert advice)
- conducting an analysis of systems to improve human performance (for example, determining how organizations learn, closing knowledge or skills gaps, and addressing human factor issues).

Change Management

TD professionals are well positioned to facilitate change because they connect people, process, and work. Change management is the capability for enabling change within an organization by using structured approaches to shift individuals, teams, and organizations from a current state to a future state. Once initiated, change follows its own nonlinear path in response to uncertainties, reactions, and guidance from those involved. There are tools, resources, processes, skills, and principles for managing the people side of change that practitioners should understand and implement to achieve preferred outcomes. Research shows that most companies don't manage change well, which makes capability in this area a differentiator for TD professionals.

> **THOUGHT LEADER VOICES**
>
> We need to help organizations decide what results they want out of the change effort they are going through.
> —Bill Rothwell, President, Rothwell & Associates

Key Knowledge Areas

A TD professional with capability in this area will need knowledge of:

- how change impacts people and organizations
- change management theories and models (for example, Lewin, Kotter, Bridges' transition model, Kubler-Ross change curve, and appreciative inquiry).

Key Capabilities

An effective TD professional will need skill in:

- assessing risk, resistance, and consequences to define a change management approach
- designing and implementing an organizational change strategy.

Data & Analytics

Data and analytics are key drivers for organizational performance and should be drivers for talent development. This is about the ability to collect, analyze, and use large data sets in real time to affect learning, performance, and business. Discerning meaningful insights from data and analytics about talent, including performance, retention, engagement, and learning, enables the talent development function to be leveraged as a strategic partner in achieving organizational goals.

Key Knowledge Areas

A TD professional with capability in this area will need knowledge of:

- the principles and applications of analytics (for example, big data, predictive modeling, data mining, machine learning, and business intelligence)
- data visualization, including principles, methods, types, and applications (for example, texture and color mapping, data representation, graphs, and word clouds)
- statistical theory and methods, including the computation, interpretation, and reporting of statistics.

Key Capabilities

An effective TD professional will need skill in:

- identifying stakeholders' needs, goals, requirements, questions, and objectives to develop a framework or plan for data analysis
- gathering and organizing data from internal or external sources in logical and practical ways to support retrieval and manipulation
- analyzing and interpreting the results of data analyses to identify patterns, trends, and relationships among variables
- selecting or using data visualization techniques (for example, flow charts, graphs, plots, word clouds, and heat maps).

Future Readiness

The pace of change requires constant upskilling and reskilling of the workforce. Future readiness requires intellectual curiosity and constant scanning of the environment to stay abreast of forces shaping the business world, employees and their expectations, and the talent development profession. Monitoring emerging trends and technologies is essential to prepare for the demands of future learners. A commitment to continuous professional development is essential to ensure there is capability to handle the changes in how work is done in the years ahead. Fostering environments that promote innovation and creativity will help position organizations become future focused.

Key Knowledge Areas

A TD professional with capability in this area will need knowledge of:

- internal and external factors that influence talent development (for example, organizational and business strategies, availability of labor, developments in other industries, societal trends, and technological advances)

- techniques to promote, support, or generate innovation and creativity (for example, design thinking, brainstorming, and ideation)
- emerging learning technologies and support systems (for example, collaborative learning software, learning management systems, authoring tools, and social media)
- information-seeking strategies and techniques.

Key Capabilities

An effective TD professional will need skill in

- conducting environmental scanning to identify current and emerging trends in the economy, legislation, competition, and technology
- applying one's own previous learning to future experiences.

4

Applying the ATD Capability Model

Competency and capability models are useful tools for individual and organizational planning because they go beyond the superficial what-people-do information conveyed in job descriptions and job analysis approaches, and convey the specific knowledge and skills individuals need to complete tasks in a way that links to organizational goals and strategies (Campion et al. 2011). This level of specificity enables individuals and organizations to take a more targeted approach to identifying skills gaps and determining the appropriate path to proficiency.

Through four decades of competency research, ATD has been committed to defining standards of practice for the community of learning and talent professionals around the globe. The 2004 study, *Mapping the Future: New Workplace Learning and Performance Competencies,* was not only a landmark for the way it defined the profession in the context of its strategic contribution to organizational performance, but also in how it was leveraged to create an ecosystem of aligned professional development and certification offerings, including self-assessment tools, certificate courses, resource guides, and professional certification. The ATD Certification Institute introduced its first certification in 2006 as a means of validating proficiency in the competencies.

By integrating new realities like technological advancements, the emergence of social media applications, and increasing globalization, the 2013 competency model advanced this mission, providing a clearly defined set of necessary knowledge, skills, abilities, and behaviors across the entire scope of the training and development profession. ATD continued to use the model to plan professional development and certification to help practitioners address knowledge and skills gaps and demonstrate proficiency against the standard. The model also provided guidance to the global community of professionals charged with linking learning, development, and performance to strategic outcomes in the workplace. From multinational corporations, businesses of all sizes, academic institutions, public sector agencies, consultants, talent development industry suppliers, and local ATD chapters, countless entities have leveraged past models as a means of benchmarking standards of excellence.

The ATD Capability Model: The Legacy Continues

The ATD Capability Model, and the 2019 ATD Competency Study it was based on, captures and codifies, for the first time, the standard of performance and quality for talent development, the name by which the profession is now known. It builds on the legacy of past studies with its comprehensive occupational study of an entire profession, as opposed to only specific jobs or roles. However, the 2019 research layered on the added objective of defining talent development and determining the ownership and scope of influence practitioners in the field have on individual and organizational outcomes. Another desired outcome of the study was to find ways to enable organizational leaders to use the model to determine the planning and design of talent development departments or functions.

> **THOUGHT LEADER VOICES**
>
> As talent developers, we need to create an organizational culture that's an inclusive and productive environment. Talent development also involves acquiring, motivating, and rewarding talent to make sure they stay with us.
> —Jack Phillips, Chairman, ROI Institute

The resulting ATD Capability Model defines what TD professionals need to know and be able to do to be successful in their jobs in the current global work environment and the near future. It demonstrates how talent development is a primary mechanism for driving performance, productivity, and operational excellence, and shows how talent development may complement or enhance traditional human resources functional areas and set a standard for talent development. The model can be used to:

- Establish a common language and consistent way to communicate about the profession.
- Convey the scope of the profession to those exploring career or professional development.
- Demonstrate the value of talent development to organizational leaders and the workforce at large.

- Enable assessment of current knowledge and skills against proficiency standards.
- Support the creation of professional development plans to address knowledge and skills gaps.
- Establish the basis for professional certification.
- Assist with the design and structuring of talent development jobs, departments, and functions.
- Guide appraisal and development of talent development staff.
- Provide insight into what talent development capabilities are needed by line managers, subject matter experts, and other nonpractitioners who are responsible for developing or educating others.

The Value Is in Application

A model that defines the standard of excellence helps lead the profession by empowering professionals to elevate their skills and enabling organizations to strategically align learning and talent development opportunities to business outcomes. However, the real utility of a capability model is in its application. Practitioners and organizations must invest in skill-building opportunities, quantify the importance and impact of talent development, and boost their credibility within the organizational landscape.

With a broad strategic imperative, talent development complements and supplements other organizational functions to prepare and enable the workforce to achieve the strategic aims of the business. Talent development clearly owns specific functions through engagement in their direct execution (such as training, performance improvement, and career development), but it also influences the broader talent management and HR ecosystem (such as talent acquisition, selection, succession planning, engagement, and performance management). It is important that TD professionals align their work— underpinned by the domains and capabilities outlined in the ATD Capability Model—to the human resource system in their or their clients' organization.

How to Apply the Model

The ATD Capability Model can be applied in a variety of ways by a diverse set of stakeholders. Individuals may use the model to explore job or career expansion, or to help prepare for professional certification. Academic institutions, professional groups, and others involved in educating those who will perform talent development functions may use the model to benchmark and align their curricula. And talent development managers and leaders may use the model to establish which roles they need to fill and which skill sets are required of their staff. Each stakeholder group will have different needs in relation to how they use the model.

Applications for Individuals

Professionals come to talent development from a number of perspectives. The field is home to those who:

- are not yet in the profession but have some existing knowledge or experience in educating others
- are currently working in a specific talent development role and want to develop further mastery of that job function
- want to increase their scope of responsibility within talent development or want to expand into a new role
- support multiple talent development functions as a part of their role
- are in a non–talent development role but occasionally perform talent development functions in addition to their core responsibilities.

Regardless of one's specific job role or context, the model can be a powerful resource for development and career planning by answering the question, "What must I know and do to be successful now and in the future?" By outlining the capability domains and key knowledge and skills requirements within, the model puts forth all the components of the profession and enables professionals to assess against those components to identify gaps.

A potential application of the model is to determine proficiency in one, several, or every capability. For example, individuals could use the sample self-assessment in Table 4-1 to measure their proficiency in the learning sciences capability. Powered by the knowledge of their own proficiency, individuals can then go in several directions, including learning and skill development, career planning, and professional credentialing.

Table 4-1. Sample Learning Sciences Capability Self-Assessment

Fill in the assessment by marking your proficiency in each of the key knowledge areas and capabilities for learning sciences.

Not applicable means the knowledge area or capability does not apply, no to little proficiency means you have little to no knowledge or skill in this area, limited proficiency indicates an incomplete knowledge or skill, and consistent proficiency means you can reliably apply knowledge or performance skill in the area. Advanced proficiency means you can apply in-depth knowledge and skill in the area, and you may lead or direct others in applying the knowledge or performing the skill. Exceptional proficiency indicates that you can apply comprehensive, expert knowledge and provide consultation or leadership to others on performing the skill.

	Learning Sciences Capability					
	Not Applicable	No to Little Proficiency	Limited Proficiency	Consistent Proficiency	Advanced Proficiency	Exceptional Proficiency
Key Knowledge Areas						
Knowledge of communication theories and models and how they relate to learning						
Knowledge of the principles and applications of cognitive science for learning (for example, auditory and visual processing, information storage and retrieval, memory, and cognitive load)						
Knowledge of the theories and models of adult learning (for example, Knowles' Adult Learning Theory, Bloom's Taxonomy, Gagne's Nine Levels of Learning, Mager's Criterion-Referenced Instruction Approach, social and collaborative learning, and experiential learning)						
Knowledge of the foundational learning theories of behaviorism, cognitivism, and constructivism						
Key Capabilities						
Skill in applying the principles of cognitive science and adult learning to design solutions that maximize learning or behavioral outcomes (for example, enhancing motivation and increasing knowledge retention)						

Learning & Skill Development

Once individuals identify their knowledge and skills gaps, they can map these gaps to specific training and education offerings that can help close them. Many professionals find it useful to build a professional development action plan they can pursue over time. Individuals may consult their managers to help select the offerings that most closely align individual development needs to the organization's priorities; these plans are commonly captured during the individual development plan (IDP) process. Some organizations even connect education and professional development activities to the performance appraisal process. Being aware of the benchmarked standard of performance may help improve an individuals' motivation and retention in professional development activities (Lasse 2015).

Career Planning

The self assessment can also help uncover how a professional's career might evolve over time and what jobs they might want to pursue in the future. Whether one is in talent development already or endeavors to enter the field, the model illustrates the full scope of the profession and which options exist for certain specialty or focus areas, as well as how to expand one's focus to more strategic activities that will drive organizational results. Individuals can use the model to conduct job research broadly or within their existing organization and to evaluate the types of job functions that exist, such as:

- internal practitioner with a focus on a particular capability, such as training delivery or instructional design
- consultant or supplier for the talent development industry
- manager or leader of a talent development function
- professionals who serve a variety of talent development functions in a generalist role.

Professional Credentialing

The model forms the foundation by which ATD's Certification Institute (ATD CI) talent development certification offerings are built. The 23 capabilities in the model are what a testing candidate would be assessed against to determine if they had the requisite knowledge and skills needed to demonstrate mastery. ATD CI currently offers two professional credentials for talent development. Visit td.org/Certification to learn more.

Note, however, that the model is not designed for a one-size-fits-all approach, and few can master every element of it. Thus, it is useful to discuss how to apply the model to one's specific context and objectives. Individuals may want to ask themselves:

- What are the skills required for the role I am currently in?
- What skills will I need to be successful as my role evolves?
- What skills will I need to be successful as my organization evolves?
- What skills will I need to align to evolutions in my industry?
- What jobs may I want to pursue in the future?
- What skills and credentials will I need to pursue my career aspirations?

TD professionals can use Table 4-2 to help establish priorities for their professional development using the domains and capabilities of the model.

Table 4-2. Priority Map for the ATD Capability Model

Domain and Capability	Present or Future? (check one or both)		Importance of Building Your Knowledge and Skill in Each Capability				
	Present	Future	0 Not Applicable	1 Not at All Important	2 Somewhat Important	3 Important	4 Very Important
Developing Personal Capability							
Communication							
Emotional Intelligence & Decision Making							
Collaboration & Leadership							
Cultural Awareness & Inclusion							
Project Management							
Compliance & Ethical Behavior							
Lifelong Learning							
Building Professional Capability							
Learning Sciences							
Instructional Design							
Training Delivery & Facilitation							
Technology Application							
Knowledge Management							
Career & Leadership Development							
Coaching							
Evaluating Impact							
Impacting Organizational Capability							
Business Insight							
Consulting & Business Partnering							
Organization Development & Culture							
Talent Strategy & Management							
Performance Improvement							
Change Management							
Data & Analytics							
Future Readiness							

As part of the customizable approach inherent to a field as broad and diverse a talent development, ATD created an interactive and customizable version of the Capability Model, which you can access via TD.org. Use this interactive model to identify the capabilities required and any knowledge or skills gaps you have for your current role, as well as what you envision for your future.

Once you identify the capabilities you need, those you have, and those you need to build, create a learning and development plan for yourself. The interactive Capability Model will link you to education courses, publications, and other ATD tools and resources that will help you close those gaps. There are a variety of resources available so you can find content that fits your learning preferences and available time and budget. Share your plan with your manager, coach, mentor, or other knowledgeable person who can help support and motivate you in your journey to expand your capabilities.

> **THOUGHT LEADER VOICES**
>
> People are innovators and innovation is the key to competitive advantage. Talent development is the key to a person's ability to innovate by providing the skill sets they need.
> —Bill Rothwell, President, Rothwell & Associates

The most important aspect of using the ATD Capability Model is to continue using it to elevate your skills and keep pace with changes in the profession.

Applications for Organizations

The ATD Capability Model is flexible and adaptable, enabling a wide range of organizations to implement it to develop their teams. Organizations recognize that talent is in short supply and demand is increasing. The speed, expectations, and complexity of work are increasing. People are staying at organizations for fewer years and may be looking at positions as stepping stones rather than careers. Meanwhile, organizations are reshaping in response to changing business models and emerging technologies. In fact, technology may be one of the biggest factors driving and enabling changes in how work is done, what employees expect from their employers, and how organizations achieve competitive advantage. Having a highly skilled talent development team can help an organization prepare to meet these challenges.

The Capability Model may be a useful framework for leaders at multiple levels—from a manager of a talent development team to a senior talent leader to a C-suite executive—because it provides insight into the range of functions talent development performs in the organization. It also articulates how professionals serving in these roles can add significant value to the organization through their work in fostering learning, improving performance, and supporting the organization through change.

Leaders can use the model to support discussions about the value of upskilling the TD team by demonstrating the link between talent development and organizational performance (Table 4-3). When TD professionals are focused on the future needs of the organization and being partners in creating that strategy, learners and the organization both win. Creating this level of employee engagement has long-term benefits.

Table 4-3. Communication Talking Points About Skill Development Across the Organization

Stakeholder	Benefit	Potential Communication Points
Executive	• Business agility • Competitiveness • ROI	• Identify competitors or market leaders who have an outward maturity in skills you've identified as gaps within the organization. • Talk with operations leaders to determine how far short of deliverables you will be if the business fails to address skills gaps; share this information with leadership. • Identify the ROI for learning programs by examining the cost to reskill or upskill an employee versus hiring one externally.
Talent Development and Human Resources Leaders	• Employee engagement • Retention	• Work with HR to understand how many employees typically leave due to lack of career growth; then hypothesize what portion may have stayed if a strategic upskilling program was in place. • To support the business case, examine engagement data for any indicators that employees are looking for more growth opportunities. (Comments and survey data are a good place to start.)
Managers	• Individual performance • Team performance	• Work with a group of managers to understand what degree of insight they have into their team members' skills and where they fall short of identified targets. • Share a wireframe of the skills gaps the TD team identified to get managers' input; this enables them to be part of the solution, especially if coaching or other high-touch training is needed.
Employees	• Job growth • Career growth	• Gather a focus group of employees to gain their insights on the market, contacts at competitors, and any personal or workforce skills gaps they see. • Use your skills gap wireframe to identify where certain types of employees could quickly close gaps and grow their abilities as well as progress toward mastery of a skill.

Reprinted by permission from Eubanks (2019).

The model can also serve as a template to show talent development managers and leaders what success looks like now and in the future. It can be leveraged to set performance expectations and incentivize staff to expand and enhance their skills to align to those expectations, thereby enhancing the image and credibility of the profession with business leaders. The integration of personal, professional, and organizational impact capabilities in the 2019 model makes it especially well-suited to communicate the talent development function's strategic value to the organization.

The specific ways organizational managers and leaders can use the model include:

- **Alignment to standards.** The model reflects current and emerging practices in the profession, giving leaders the opportunity to evaluate roles, resources, and priorities to ensure alignment with the standards of practice.
- **Job and organizational design.** Managers and leaders may use the model to define the roles required of a talent development department and how this function should integrate with other organizational units.
- **Learning and development planning.** Managers and leaders may use the key knowledge and skill areas for each capability in the model to assess the current skill level of TD staff and facilitate the development of IDPs to address gaps. They may also use the model to create internal training and certification programs or to recommend the appropriate learning solutions available in the marketplace.
- **Performance management.** The key knowledge and skill capability areas provide a level of specificity to establish clear terminology and expectations that can underpin performance appraisals, development planning, coaching, and feedback for talent development staff.
- **Career and succession planning.** Employees may use the model to self-assess and gain insight into current proficiency and requirements for other positions. Managers can help expand the pipeline of available talent by recommending specific development activities to help prepare employees for future roles.
- **Selection and promotion.** Managers and leaders may adapt the model to create selection criteria and aid in competency-based interviewing to improve the hiring and placement of the most qualified individuals.

Action Planning for Teams

A team assessment can be conducted to determine where to begin with applying the model within a team or department. ATD's 2018 whitepaper *Bridging the Skills Gap* identified a useful six-step process to follow:

1. Clarify and understand your organization's strategies and performance metrics.

2. Identify the skills and capabilities that map to the strategies and performance metrics.

3. Assess the knowledge and skills gaps of each person on the team.

4. Create a plan to address the gaps.

5. Implement solutions.

6. Evaluate and communicate impact.

> **THOUGHT LEADER VOICES**
>
> On an organizational scale, talent development is thinking about learning culture and strategy; on an individual scale, it's talking about specific knowledge and skill development for individual people in the organization.
>
> —Catherine Lombardozzi, Founder, Learning 4 Learning Professionals

Customizing the Model for Use in Your Organization

Once a team assessment has been conducted, talent development managers may want to fully customize the ATD Capability Model to better integrate it into their organizations. Use this checklist to guide customization decisions:

- Who are the targeted users of your capability model (what are their job roles)?
- What performance level is being targeted (good or outstanding)?
- What is the time horizon for your capability model (present, future, or both)?
- Where will your capability model be used (geographical scope)?
- Why is your capability model being used (for development only or for all uses, such as recruitment, selection, promotion, performance management, and compensation)?
- What specifics are important to reflect in your capability model (your specific industry or geographical location)?

Use the following four-phase process to help tailor the capability model to suit your use or application.

Phase 1: Create a Customized Model

First, form a team of individuals and their supervisors who represent your target group. Ideally, this group consists of good or outstanding performers. Then ask the team to review the ATD Capability Model and recommend which capabilities align with your organization's talent development strategy, mission, and specific needs. Or, consider the model in its entirety to gain a holistic view of current and desired future state proficiency.

Once you've chosen your capabilities, set up a series of meetings to discuss the knowledge and skill statements under each capability to identify which knowledge and skill the performers need to demonstrate to achieve success. The team's job is to examine, modify, and remove any knowledge or skills that are not appropriate to your organization's culture. You should end up with a very lean, targeted list.

Using the results of these meetings, the team should develop a final ideal performer profile that is appropriate for your corporate or national culture. This final product is your customized rough draft capability list.

At the end of this process, you might choose to conduct behavioral event interviews (BEIs) to ground the rough draft in the reality of your workplace. A behavioral event interview is used to collect information about past behavior, usually in a structured and prescribed format. Excellent information about BEIs can be found in *Competence at Work: Models for Superior Performance* by Lyle M. Spencer and Signe M. Spencer (1993).

Phase 2: Validate Your Rough Draft Model

The purpose of the second phase is to validate the rough draft capability list with the targeted job incumbents, their immediate supervisors, and their stakeholders.

Now that you have a rough draft of your organization's capabilities, you can validate its conclusions and recommendations by conducting a series of focus groups, retreats, or surveys. You can also take a multi-rater assessment approach by asking the performers in your target groups and their immediate supervisors if the capabilities and knowledge and skill statements are appropriate. You may also want to include other key stakeholders (such as C-suite executives and learners) in this assessment.

Before beginning the validation, develop a cut score. For instance, if raters are asked to review item importance on a five-point scale, eliminate anything that receives a rating of less than 4.5. It is better to have fewer capabilities and behaviors than too many because this will help users to focus. At the end of phase 2, you should have a final list that has been reviewed and validated.

Phase 3: Get Senior-Level Approval

Once you and your team are comfortable with your final targeted list, present it (if possible) to a formal team of upper management leaders. It is essential to secure agreement from all stakeholders that the final list is in alignment with your organization's strategic goals and current and future business needs. It is also helpful to think about how to best communicate it—consider creating a graphic that depicts the major capability areas at a high level.

Phase 4: Get Set to Use the Model

Review all elements of your organization's HR system as they relate to talent development practitioners. Pay particular attention to how the model will be applied at the outset of the project.

If you're using the model for career and skills development alone, you may want to develop assessments so you can determine the strengths and weaknesses of individual talent development practitioners. If you choose to apply the model more widely, then you will need to incorporate its contents into all elements of your performance management system (including recruitment, selection, development, performance appraisals, and promotions). The interactive capability model at TD.org can help each team member perform a self-assessment against the knowledge and skills statements that apply to them or your team.

A Few Customization Caveats

Any effort to create a capability model for your organization must be approached thoughtfully. First, note that each step of the tailoring process should be done in a way that is legally defensible. Different nations have different laws, rules, and regulations governing employment. Be sure to consult legal counsel in your locale to ensure that your adaption is legally defensible.

Second, each step of the tailoring process should be the focus of a communication plan that parallels—and is as robust as—the technical plan.

Third, remember that globally oriented companies may need to review the model in different geographical locations or regions around the world to localize the content.

While the capabilities may remain the same, different regional may need adjustments in required behaviors.

Applications for Educators and Industry Groups

Academic institutions, training companies, professional associations, industry groups, and consultants and suppliers to the talent development community are part of the vast network of individuals and organizations helping to advance the profession through education. Their efforts to help professionals network with industry peers, expand their skills, and earn credentials have gained prominence as support for lifelong learning grows. ATD's 2018 research report *Lifelong Learning: The Path to Personal and Organizational Performance* shows a correlation between continuous learning and organizational performance, enhanced ability to respond to changing business needs, and greater competitive ability.

These entities may use the model to communicate priorities, plan curricula, and create learning programs. Specifically, educators may use the model to:

- Assess learners' needs by measuring current skills against the capabilities in the model.
- Communicate about the scope and value of talent development.
- Evaluate existing course offerings to determine which aspects of the model to incorporate.
- Update existing course offerings to include broader coverage of the capabilities in the model.
- Develop new course offerings to develop knowledge and skills the capabilities in the model.
- Align an entire curriculum around the capabilities in the model.

A Note About ATD Chapters

Affiliate groups help extend the reach of ATD in U.S. localities and in regions around the globe. Chapters serve as a means for TD professionals to share information, network, and enhance their skills through education opportunities. Similar to educational institutions, ATD chapters can use the model to assess the proficiency of their constituents and create professional development programming to address gaps. Chapters may even use the model to create an annual programming plan, ensuring coverage on an array of capabilities that align to the roles and skill requirements of their members. The model could also be used to support chapter members who want to pursue a talent development certification through ATD. By offering information, study groups, and mentorship, ATD chapters may connect the local community of professionals with the resources available to them to pursue their career aspirations.

Taking the Next Step

It's well worth repeating that while the ATD Capability Model can serve an informational role in capturing what is most needed among TD professionals now and in the future, its value stems from its potential application. It has been designed for individuals and organizations to place themselves in its center and apply or customize it to their needs. Chapter 5 offers some examples of how individuals, chapters, and organizations have put competency and capability models into action.

5

Examples of Applying the ATD Capability Model

Chapter 4 explained how individuals, teams, organizations, and others can apply the model. Individual contributors will want to use the model as a guide to understanding the full scope and breadth of talent development. Regardless of the type of role someone has, the size of the organization, the industry, or the location, the model can be used as a tool for an individual's career development plan. Similarly, managers or consultants can use the model to help talent development teams identify areas of strength, opportunities for growth, and activities or resources that can support the team's knowledge and skills development.

What does that look like in action? Who has put a capability model to work? Let's review the perspectives of other TD professionals who have used previous ATD models to develop themselves, their peers, and their teams.

A Professional Road Map to Navigate the Future

With 20 years of experience in talent development, Chris Coladonato has used ATD models for several things: to learn more when she was transitioning into the field initially, as she planned her professional development and career goals, and to prepare and study for the Certified Professional in Learning and Performance credential that she earned in 2011.

"I was able to evaluate the areas [competencies] I felt I was good at and areas I wanted to explore further, and, with those two things, I had a better sense of the road map for my career," explains Chris of using the 2004 ASTD Model to assess her strengths and interests. "Supporting and leveraging the curation of knowledge in our field is a foundational skill. We should all know how to do it and help others understand how to do it. If you have those skills, you will go much further, faster."

"Competency models and capability maps are underutilized," she continues. "Whatever your profession is, if there is a model, it's something you can leverage for your own personal development and road map. . . . it's a guide. Ultimately, how do you know where you're going in your career unless you have a good grasp on where the field is going? A capability model is one way to understand that.

"Learning about the ATD model shouldn't be a once and done," Chris says. "As an important tool in your career development, you should revisit the model at least every year because things that were not important to you or critical to your career in the past may be of interest to you today or tomorrow. It's a professional road map to navigate the future."

Leverage the ATD Model As a Guiding Resource

Jennifer Brink is the senior director of L&D Talent Development at Comcast, a large global media and technology company headquartered in Philadelphia, Pennsylvania. Comcast University (CU), the learning enterprise responsible for delivering learning and development to Comcast's employee base, also has the responsibility of developing its training staff to ensure that they are delivering a learning experience that meets the needs of learners and the demands of the business.

Jennifer notes that CU developed its own competency model six years ago using the 2013 ASTD model as a reference and a resource. CU's model sets the foundation for trainer development, courses, and development experiences, and it's also core to CU's internal trainer certification program. Many of Comcast's trainers come from within the company—especially from one of the call centers or in-field operations—and they leverage CU's model as a baseline for their knowledge and skills. "With the competency model, our trainers become well versed on their role, the responsibilities, and the expectations of being a trainer at Comcast," Jennifer says.

In addition, CU leverages its model for managers who assess CU trainers through observation—it is the basis for observing skills and behaviors that a trainer demonstrates while teaching a CU course. Jennifer notes that managers use the competency model as the basis for their guidance and feedback for trainers, and to identify opportunities for further development.

As delivery methods have evolved to include learning online and social learning, CU's model has evolved as well. Jennifer says that additional skills and behaviors have been added to the model that are relevant to the learning delivery methods as they continue to change based on the needs of learners and the business.

Use a Model to Assess Where You Are and Where You Want to Go

Stephanie Hubka, CPLP, has used previous ATD models in a variety of ways, pointing out that sometimes it's the simplest thing you can do that have the greatest impact.

When Stephanie started a new job in 2011, around the time she earned the CPLP credential, the only item she hung in her workspace was a poster of the ASTD Competency Model. She was part of a small team and the poster encouraged conversation about the model. Over time, members of the team would ask how they could learn more about a specific area of the competency model, and later they asked to review it at an upcoming staff meeting.

"It became a common reference point and language that all members of our team shared about our profession, the work we were doing together, and areas that what we wished we could learn more about," recalls Stephanie. "I always keep a copy of the ATD model hanging near my desk."

> **THOUGHT LEADER VOICES**
>
> Talent development creates value by being aware of and aligned with the strategic goals of the organization and then preparing people to reach those strategic goals.
> —Karl Kapp, Professor and Consultant, Bloomsburg University, Institute for Interactive Technologies

Having a conversation about the model with a colleague or individual on your team can turn into an opportunity for personal growth. For example, Stephanie says that even if a person has limited knowledge or experience in the profession, they can begin establishing themselves as an emerging leader: "I suggest to colleagues that you don't have to be an expert in every area. With expertise in one or more areas, you can emerge as a leader in the subjects you do know as you continue to build your knowledge in other areas."

At the team level, Stephanie advises that competency and capability models present an opportunity for teams to talk about where they see themselves today, assess their gaps in knowledge and performance, and prioritize how they can learn together.

"Then, decide where you want to focus your efforts and time." Stephanie recommends thinking about it in this way: "Who is good at what areas and who can teach one another about other areas?"

Today, in her work as a managing partner for Protos Learning, Stephanie always begins her client engagements with a discussion about what success looks like, and she uses the ATD model to frame the initial conversation.

"I want my clients and their teams to be familiar with the model because I use it as an important reference tool for projects I am doing on their behalf," she explains. "It allows us to have a shared understanding of important concepts and practices in our field."

Use Competencies to Select and Develop Talent

Seema Nagrath Menon, CPLP, leads the Center for Action in Learning Management (CALM Worldwide), a management and learning consultancy based in Dubai, the United Arab Emirates. Seema notes that as a growing organization, "a focus on skills without looking at the broader competencies will not be enough to develop and drive career development for employees."

CALM Worldwide used the 2013 ASTD model "as a framework to help focus our employees' behavior on things that matter most to the organization, which in turn helps drive success and growth," says Seema. "We also use competencies to select and develop talent for our organization."

In addition, Seema and her team use the ATD model to effectively implement the use of competencies with clients "because it is future-focused and covers areas that are relevant to success for businesses. The competencies in the ATD model are organized in a logical framework which helped us in our consultation."

"[CALM Worldwide] aligned the competencies in the ATD model to the overall strategic focus of our client organizations to ensure it is relevant to help them achieve excellence," Seema explains. "As TD practitioners we also used this model as a road map for our own professional development and to create individual learning plans. And, we used it to develop the right talent and TD competencies for our consultancy."

Align Professional Development Opportunities With a Competency-Based Approach

Several ATD chapters used previous ATD models to plan professional development programs, regional conferences, and networking events—all with the purpose of helping their members learn more about the knowledge and skills required for success in each area of the model. Here are several examples of how ATD chapters used the most recent ATD model to help their members learn and grow.

ATD Los Angeles Chapter: Brain Exchange and New Year Networking Mixer

The ATD Los Angeles Chapter organized a new year networking mixer that gave local professionals an opportunity to exchange ideas, showcase their talents, and connect with one another. Facilitators asked attendees to come prepared to share a tip, tool, or piece of advice that they had implemented at their workplaces with a 90-second time limit. As a bonus, attendees explained how their tips tied into an area of expertise from the ATD model. Overall, the event enabled the chapter to reengage its membership while balancing the capabilities of a small leadership team. As a result of the mixer, the chapter gained 19 new members and sold out its program for the month.

ATD Cascadia Chapter: Conference Speakers Selection Process

The ATD Cascadia Chapter in Portland, Oregon, hosts an annual conference for local and regional TD professionals. Several years ago, the chapter's conference team developed and implemented an automated request for proposals (RFP) to gather a pool of potential session speakers for the conference. Each speaker was required to include a video clip of a presentation similar to their proposed topic. Included in the RFP form were questions about how the speaker's presentation aligned with the ATD model. By including these questions on the RFP, chapter was able to provide more targeted conference sessions as well as the information attendees needed to document continuing education credits.

ATD Hawaii Chapter: Event Stamp Card With Areas of Expertise

Following the release of the 2013 ATD model, the ATD Hawaii chapter planned more than 10 events connected to the areas of expertise (AOEs). Providing a stamp card (similar to a passport), the chapter encouraged its members to "sharpen their swords" in the 10 AOEs by attending at least one event in each area. Those who attended all 10 events during the year received a certificate of completion and were entered into a year-end drawing.

ATD Buffalo Niagara Chapter: Monthly Member Webcasts

To provide an engaging experience for all members of the chapter, especially those who found it challenging to attend monthly in-person meetings, the ATD Buffalo Niagara Chapter shifted its programming to monthly, recorded webcasts. Using webinar technology, the chapter was able to present a variety of speakers addressing different areas of the ATD model. Since the presentations were recorded, the chapter was able to develop a webcast archive for members, which increased the value of membership. Through the change, the chapter gained new members and now provides a wider variety of topics and programming.

Now It's Your Turn

There are many opportunities for organizations to apply the ATD Capability Model within their talent development function. In this chapter, we've provided several examples of how the model can help individuals and teams foster their own knowledge and skill development in unique ways. It's important to remember that one size does not fit every team or organization. A review of the model and an assessment of what's most important for your talent development function and organization must be considered before tackling this important exercise.

Visit td.org/CapabilityModel for more resources and tools on implementing and customizing the model for your organization.

A Call to Action for the Talent Development Profession

Talent development professionals are future-focused, key contributors to the success of an organization's mission. As illustrated in the 2019 Competency Study, TD professionals are uniquely positioned to respond to the trends affecting the field, including the rapid availability of information, big data, and the digital transformation. As organizations are changed by artificial intelligence and automation, part-time and contract workers, virtual and remote work, and other factors, TD professionals can leverage their diverse skill set to unleash human potential to drive learning and results.

The knowledge, skills, and abilities outlined in the ATD Capability Model demonstrate that talent development fuels organizational performance, productivity, and results. TD professionals do this by creating the processes, systems, and frameworks that foster learning, leveraging technology and innovation to maximize individual performance, and collaborating with business leaders to align development activities to strategic business outcomes.

The model provides a framework for TD professionals to grow and expand their skills over the entire arc of their career. It also provides a road map for what practitioners must do to remain competitive. Key actions for TD professionals include:

- **Being an advocate for a culture of lifelong learning for others and themselves.** TD professionals need to remain diligent about enhancing and expanding their own knowledge and skills to align with evolutions in technology, artificial intelligence, learning science, and global economic factors. This includes embracing lifelong learning for themselves and modeling the best way to stay abreast of trends and environmental factors. TD professionals can serve as leaders in this area and help prepare their organizations to take advantage of the opportunities the future will hold. ATD research found that "more than two-thirds of TD leaders said improved engagement was the leading benefit their organizations expected to gain from encouraging lifelong learning. Other most-anticipated returns included better organizational performance, improved talent retention, enhanced ability to respond to changing business needs, and greater competitive ability. Lower-performing organizations were likely to look at lifelong learning as a potential means of enhancing change-response capabilities" (ATD 2018).

- **Connecting talent development to organizational strategies and quantifiable impact metrics.** TD professionals need to enhance their ability to communicate how talent development contributes to organizations, develop a greater focus on strategic planning, and show measurable

> **THOUGHT LEADER VOICES**
>
> A talent development professional realizes they could execute training or do a variety of other things that are backed up by solid information, subject matter expertise, research, or data.
> —JD Dillon, Chief Learning Architect, Axonify

  behavior change. Learning to communicate with business leaders about the why of a solution and its measurable impact will better position talent development as a partner in organizational success.

- **Expanding the talent development positioning around how learning occurs.** As information becomes more accessible and available in a variety of forms, and industries require a rapid pace of upskilling, TD professionals need to expand an organization's understanding of the types of learning that can enhance an employee's performance. This includes creating a system of knowledge management, conceptualizing, managing, and maintaining organizational knowledge, and incorporating formal and informal learning and carefully curated content.

- **Partnering with senior leadership, line managers, and HR to create an integrated talent strategy.** TD professionals are in a key position to help an organization be proactive versus reactive, developing the kind of skilled workforce that is needed at just the right time. This approach creates a competitive advantage for organizations and better readies them for the future of work.

Keeping the ATD Capability Model Current

The traditional timeline for updating previous ATD competency models has been every five to seven years to keep pace with changes in the profession. The most recent study demonstrated that the pace of change is increasing, and more frequent updating may be required to reflect the capabilities needed to be a successful talent development professional.

When developing the new capability model, ATD paid special attention to building a framework that was evergreen and could serve as a more stable but adaptable construct that reflects what TD professionals do. This will allow for more frequent updating of how the work is done. The model's flexibility will allow TD professionals to reshape it for themselves as their job role or career grows and changes, identifying new capabilities that can be developed for continued growth.

> **THOUGHT LEADER VOICES**
>
> I look at talent development as the lever that drives operational excellence in organizations.
> —Patti Phillips, CEO, ROI Institute

ATD is committed to making ongoing enhancements to incorporate new methodologies and concepts as they emerge in response to the profession's evolution. Through an ongoing review process, ATD will more frequently conduct the environmental scanning and identification of trends influencing the field. These emerging concepts will be explored through education content, validated through pulse check surveys, and, if confirmed as an additional capability, added to the model.

The flexibility and adaptability of ATD's Capability Model provides a framework for all TD professionals, whether they are subject matter experts who have just been asked to train colleagues, a long-tenured instructional designer, a chief talent development officer, or a newly promoted manager learning to develop their team. Identifying a personal capability model or the best model to develop your team will enable TD professionals to unleash their own potential to develop successful teams and organizations.

A Call to Action

The new ATD Capability Model has been comprehensively researched and validated. This future-oriented, adaptable, and customizable model leverages the role of talent development for organizational success. The model encourages TD professionals and their organizations to keep their skills current and provides a road map to make that happen. In general terms, practitioners are advised to:

- Update their knowledge of new and emerging technologies and how they apply to the talent development profession.
- Model the importance of lifelong learning and creating learning cultures within their organizations.
- Commit to learning more about trends affecting the future of work and the talent implications they carry.
- Expand their understanding of data and how to analyze and apply it.
- Continue to deepen understanding of the three domains of practice and 23 capabilities.
- Leverage the unique blending of capabilities across the three domains to enhance their personal practice as a TD professional and the value the talent development function can bring to the organization.
- Continue to align talent development efforts with organizational goals and use strategic metrics to demonstrate talent development's contribution to organizational success.

The talent development profession is adapting to disruptions in the global marketplace. It has never been more critical for TD professionals to become key partners in helping ensure organizations are prepared for the future. Implementing the ATD Capability Model for yourself and your team means developing your own capabilities so that you can leverage your expanding portfolio of professional expertise to help the organizations you serve realize their full potential.

Appendix A
The Research Behind the ATD Capability Model

To better understand the ATD Capability Model, how you fit in, and how you might apply it, you need to see some of the background research that shaped it. Like with all previous competency models, ATD and its partners conducted extensive research before developing the ATD Capability Model. The competency model project began with a literature review and environmental scan of trends affecting the profession. Interviews with key thought leaders highlighted themes, which echoed the trends uncovered. From there, ATD collaborated with subject matter experts to write knowledge and skill statements that defined the profession. To gather hard data on the relevance of these statements, ATD circulated them in a survey along with demographic questions to TD professionals. A brief overview of the knowledge, skills, and abilities (KSA) results can be found in chapter 3, and the full data are reported in Appendix C.

Trends Research

The foundation of the capability model research entailed capturing the major shifts in society and the larger business landscape since the previous model was published. The major changes in our field were identified through a comprehensive literature review, expert practitioner interviews, and Advisory Panel discussions. These trends spanned a variety of areas in business, technology, learning, science, and the profession itself, and were directly incorporated into the research to determine their impact on future skill requirements for practitioners.

The most notable finding from the trends research was that talent development no longer focuses solely on the tactical aspects of the design and delivery of learning. Instead, the TD field has become a key element in the success and competitive advantage of organizations, making its practitioners essential partners with all areas of a business in achieving organizational goals.

Business Trends

A key business trend concerns the changing profile of the worker. Successive genera-tions are entering the workforce with increasing global awareness of cultural and social differ-ences, environmental challenges, and attitudes about work. Many young workers expect their employers to be not just successful enterprises providing meaningful work experiences, but also good corporate citizens.

KEY BUSINESS TRENDS
• Demographics of workers
• Contingent or gig workforce
• Digital transformation
• Innovation and adaptability

A related trend is the rapid growth of the "alternative workforce"—the contingent workforce, or as some call it, the gig economy—a labor market characterized by short-term contracts or freelance work as opposed to permanent jobs. According to the Gig Economy Data Hub, a joint project of Cornell University's Institute of Labor Rela-tions and the Aspen Institute, the percentage of contingent workers currently reaches between 25 and 30 percent of the total workforce and will continue to grow to more than a third in coming years.

While the gig economy is a boon to fast-moving entrepreneurs, it is less so to tra-ditional businesses. TD professionals note that this shift in the workforce will change what it means to be an organization and how to engage workers in its goals and purposes.

Aiding the rise of the gig economy is the digital transformation affecting all indus-tries and organizational functions. Digital transformation is causing leaders to rethink how their businesses are structured and is forcing them to go to market in entirely new ways. As a result, the entire landscape of business and work has shifted.

Because of the widespread disruption of traditional industries, innovation and adaptability are rapidly replacing production efficiency as drivers of work processes and practices. Using tools such as design thinking, firms are reimagining how to create products and engage customers.

Today, organizations need to reinvent themselves at high speed or they risk being disrupted out of existence. That means staying ahead of the game while also changing it. The talent development profession is at the center of efforts to create agile employees and new thinking in organizations facing disruption. They can deliver value by preparing organizations to collaborate across departments and reskill or upskill workers.

Technology Trends

By now, it is a given that technology disrupts but also opens doors to new ways of doing things. The ubiquity of information and the technology for finding precisely what you need has enabled TD professionals to create customized responses to learning needs and to make information more accessible, richer in content, and more adaptable. It has also expanded the learning environment

> **KEY TECHNOLOGY TRENDS**
> - Ubiquity of information
> - New means for accessing learning
> - Artificial intelligence
> - "Superjobs"

far beyond the classroom into mobile devices and virtual environments inspired by gaming and other immersive technologies. Technology has also made it easier to collect and analyze data to determine the influence of learning on performance.

The use of artificial intelligence (AI), cognitive technologies, and robotics to automate and augment work is on the rise, prompting the redesign of jobs in many domains and the skills required to do them. A 2019 report from Deloitte notes that "The jobs of today are more machine-powered and data-driven than in the past, and they also require more human skills in problem-solving, communication, interpretation, and design." The report predicts that as machines take over repeatable tasks and work becomes less routine, many jobs will become "superjobs" featuring work and responsibilities combined from multiple traditional jobs—a category that will change how organizations think about work and the skills needed by individual workers. It will also change how companies approach talent development and how they use AI and data analytics in talent development decision-making and learning design.

Learning Trends

In the early days of the training profession, it was common for adults to complete their formal education before starting work, and then to experience little structured learning beyond orientation. But as time passed, organizations gained perspective on the need to ensure that all employees had knowledge and skills throughout their careers

to achieve specific personal and organizational goals. As the value of human capital evolved, so did the training profession—expanding from the corporate classroom to the cloud. While training was seen as a series of events primarily for transferring knowledge from one person to many, talent development represents a broad set of capabilities and practices intended to drive performance and results throughout organizations.

As employee learning grows and evolves, the focus continues to shift from the competence of the trainers to the competence of the learners. Implementation is judged by how successfully a person or team can perform as a result of gaining new knowledge, and how much they increase their learning skills. Metacognition—awareness or analysis of one's own learning or thinking processes—has become part of the learner's toolkit.

Science Trends

Studies of the anatomy, physiology, and molecular biology of the human nervous system and brain are replacing decades of conjecture about

learning with research-based evidence. The talent development field has benefited from an explosion of scientific discoveries—from the way neurons influence cognition to sleep's role in our ability to learn, memorize, and make logical decisions.

New research on adult learning, cognition, memory, and behavior has filled some gaps in understanding how the structure and function of the brain influence learning. Virtual, multiplayer games reveal additional insights into how groups of players learn to reach goals together and what motivates them to learn in a game setting. Psychological research explores the processes of learning, teaching, motivation, classroom management, social interaction, communication, and assessment. Today's TD professionals use these findings to inform their work and improve their practices.

Trends in the Profession

With most aspects of business on a fast track, TD professionals are turning to accelerated learning that can be self-directed, individualized, and quickly updated. They are helping learners gain independence and control over what they're learning, which is increasingly available just in time in customized chunks.

TD professionals need critical skills such as business and technology acumen, data analysis, and content curation. They're spending more time partnering with other business units and focusing the attention of learners for maximum efficiency. Often, they lead efforts to engage people and teams to be more innovative and agile, using methods such as design thinking and adapting ideas from social network theory.

The plethora of information available through the Internet has added content curation to the talent development role. Many TD professionals are now responsible for selecting and evaluating off-the-shelf, "found" learning for its quality, applicability, and effectiveness.

In an age of artificial intelligence, TD professionals face new challenges in analyzing and interpreting data, deriving insights, and summarizing findings. AI systems can analyze vast amounts of data and make recommendations about hiring or promotions, for example, but humans are left to explain and defend these conclusions. The task of these explainers is often to communicate complex information appropriately to different kinds of audiences.

With the proliferation of data, TD professionals have new sources and means for capturing the effectiveness of their efforts. Measuring and evaluating the impact of talent development is a must-do to make a meaningful business case for the real value of investing in people. Equally important is the need for practitioners in our field to be strong advisors and partners to the managers and leaders of the businesses they serve. Data and analytics can serve as powerful tools to help talent development practitioners identify, quantify, and share insights on how talent supports organizational strategy and competitive advantage.

To keep pace with advances in the profession, the number of academic curricula and degree programs related to talent development has increased. The ATD website TD.org includes a directory of 481 academic degree programs in education, training, and adult learning; human resource management; instructional design; leadership development; organizational development; and organizational psychology. Additionally, professional education and credential programs abound, enabling the just-in-time skill development and validation of expertise that practitioners need to keep pace with continuous evolution in the field.

These and other trends that shape business, the economy, and the workforce will continue to influence the practice of talent development in the coming years.

The Occupational Survey of KSAs

The results of the trends research overwhelmingly indicated that the role of TD professionals has moved beyond the traditional realm of training design and delivery. Effective talent development requires a proactive, business-partner approach to anticipate and respond to changing needs and to leverage personal capabilities to support organizational strategy and generate competitive advantage. The trends research, literature review, and structured interviews led ATD to crafting competency statements.

Additionally, ATD wanted to determine how practitioners of talent development rated the relative importance of the statements. To do so, ATD conducted an occupational survey.

The Goal of the Occupational Survey

The primary purposes of the competency study were to identify the knowledge, skills, and abilities (KSAs) required for TD professionals to perform their roles effectively and to obtain information on career and development pathways for them. Since this was the first study done under the banner of "talent development," defining the full scope of what encompasses the field was a key goal.

To that end, the 2019 model development project would create a set of original KSA statements, rather than building on the 2013 competency framework. A task force of subject matter experts came together to write KSA statements that were designed to encompass all possible aspects of the TD professional's role. The statements they developed covered many familiar competencies such as instructional design and training delivery, as well as more specialized professional competencies, such as those related to being strategic business partners and those considered foundational or enabling interpersonal competencies.

Based on this broad new perception of the role, the knowledge and skill statements for TD professionals were less tactical and more strategic than in previous studies. The statements were also written to focus more on the "what we do" for the field than "how we do it," which allows for more frequent updating of the model to keep pace with trends and changes in the field. The occupational survey statements were designed to determine if frontline TD professionals agreed with this expanded scope of responsibilities. The resulting 197 statements, along with demographic questions, were assembled into a survey that went out to the field.

Who Responded to the Survey

More than 5,400 professionals participated in the survey, resulting in 3,033 usable responses, the largest response ever to an ATD competency study survey. A useable response is one where a person has responded to at least 56 percent of the questions. Respondents who gave the same rating to at least 90 percent of the statements were excluded from analysis.

Overall, respondents tended to be female (61 percent), between 40 and 60 years old (50 percent), based in the United States (77 percent), highly educated (90 percent), employed full-time (94 percent), and moderately experienced in talent development (>10 years; 59 percent). The sample comprised individuals from the entry-level (3 percent), specialist (43 percent), management (38 percent), and executive/C-suite (16 percent) ranks.

Nearly two-thirds of the respondents worked at for-profit U.S.-based (33 percent) or multinational (32 percent) organizations. Slightly more than half (54 percent) work at large organizations (501 to 50,000 employees). In comparison, 61 percent of the respondents reported that their talent development function included 10 or fewer staff members. While some respondents indicated that their talent development function reported to operations (18 percent) or the executive office (13 percent), the majority indicated that their function reported to human resources (52 percent). Roughly 15 percent of the people in the sample were employed by small businesses or owned their own businesses.

The respondents to the 2019 survey differed from the 2013 survey in several ways. First and foremost, there were a greater number of total respondents; 3,033 is more than double the number who responded to the prwevious survey. In addition, 23 percent of respondents came from 69 countries other than the United States, providing the largest set of global data yet. Nearly six times as many respondents were under the age of 30, potentially signaling an intention to enter the field earlier in one's career. Survey respondents also represented a larger swath of professionals in this survey, as evidenced by a significant increase in participation from those with fewer than three years of experience, and a two-fold increase in input from C-suite level executives (from 237 respondents in 2013 to nearly 500 in 2019).

How the Research Shaped the Model

The results from the competency model research, including the trend analysis and occupational survey, show how the TD profession continues to expand in focus and reach. TD professionals now touch nearly every component of the organization and the employee life cycle. They no longer wait to be asked for their input, but proactively address organizational issues to create sustainable business improvements. In addition, they are more global and diverse than ever, with survey responses from practitioners representing 70 countries.

All of this has led to a complete overhaul of the 2013 ASTD Competency Model.

Appendix B
Prior ATD Competency Studies and Key Findings

2013

ASTD Competency Study:
The Training and Development Profession Redefined

The primary goal of the 2013 ASTD Competency Study was to update the knowledge, skills, abilities, and behaviors first identified in the 2004 Competency Study. Focused interviews with 188 experienced subject matter experts and thought leaders gathered perspectives on the 2004 Competency Model, in general, and the areas of expertise (AOEs), in particular, and identified trends and developments in the field that may have affected the 2004 Competency Model. These findings were then validated through a survey that had 1,313 respondents.

Key Findings

The study resulted in changes to the actual Competency Model graphic, from the pyramid to a pentagon shape to illustrate no hierarchy in the updated model. The Study provided important insights into which competencies were emerging, transforming, and increasing in terms of their importance. Most notably:

- an emphasis on technology literacy
- adopting a global mindset
- demonstrating emotional intelligence
- developing dual industry knowledge
- being innovative.

As a result, three new AOEs were added to the model: Industry Knowledge, Technology Literacy, and Global Mindset.

Additionally, five existing AOEs were updated to incorporate learning analytics and include informal learning methods, social media, and leveraging technology:

- Designing Learning became Instructional Design
- Delivering Training became Training Delivery
- Measurement and Evaluation became Evaluating Learning Impact
- Managing Organizational Knowledge became Knowledge Management
- Career Planning and Talent Management became Integrated Talent Management.

2004
ASTD Competency Study: Mapping the Future

More than 2,000 training and development professionals and senior leaders from around the world participated in the ASTD Competency Study: Mapping the Future. The principle objectives were to identify the most significant trends and drivers that would affect current and future practice; describe a comprehensive, inspiring, and future-oriented competency model; and provide a foundation for competency-based applications, deliverables, and outputs—including certification.

Key Findings

The study identified eight key trends for which training and development professionals should prepare:

- drastic times, drastic measures
- blurred lines—life or work
- small world and shrinking
- new faces, new expectations
- work be nimble, work be quick
- security alert!
- life and work in the e-lane
- a higher ethical bar.

The study identified three major categories (clusters) of foundational competencies, four key roles associated with each category—intrapersonal, business/management, and personal—and nine major areas of expertise (AOEs) needed by training and development professionals:

- Designing Training
- Improving Human Performance
- Delivering Training
- Measuring and Evaluating
- Facilitating Organizational Change
- Managing the Learning Function
- Coaching
- Managing Organizational Knowledge
- Career Planning and Talent Management.

1999
ASTD Models for Workplace Learning and Performance

Practitioners, senior practitioners, and line managers provided input for the *ASTD Models for Workplace Learning and Performance* report to determine what current and future competencies (five years beyond 1999) would be required to succeed in the field. The report defined workplace learning and performance as "the integrated use of learning and other interventions for the purpose of improving individual and organizational performance."

Key Findings

This report defined roles (not job titles) as "a grouping of competencies targeted to meet specific expectations of a job or function" (Rothwell et al. 1999). Seven workplace learning and performance roles were identified, including manager, analyst, intervention selector, intervention designer, intervention implementor, change leader, and evaluator.

In addition, 52 specific competencies were identified and classified into six groups:

- **Analytical competencies**—the creation of new understandings or methods through the synthesis of multiple ideas, processes, and data

- **Technical competencies**—the understanding and application of existing knowledge or processes
- **Leadership competencies**—influencing, enabling, or inspiring others to act
- **Business competencies**—understanding organizations as systems and the processes, decision criteria, and issues that businesses face
- **Interpersonal competencies**—understanding and applying methods that produce effective interactions between people and groups
- **Technological competencies**—understanding and applying current, new, or emerging technologies.

1998
ASTD Models for Learning Technologies

The *ASTD Models for Learning Technologies* report examined the roles, competencies, and work outputs that human resource development (HRD) professionals need to implement learning technologies in their organizations. HRD professionals were identified as those who use training and development, organization development, and career development to improve individual, group, and organizational effectiveness.

Key Findings
The 1998 study provided a classification system that related instructional methods (lectures, role plays, and simulations) to presentation methods (computer-based training, electronic performance support systems, multimedia, and video) and distribution formats (audiotape, CD-ROM, Internet, and videotape; Piskurich and Sanders 1998).

1996
ASTD Models for Human Performance Improvement

The *ASTD Models for Human Performance Improvement* (HPI) report explored the roles, competencies, and outputs that human performance improvement professionals (or performance consultants) need to create meaningful change within organizations. The report presented HPI as a process, not a discipline. For example, instructional systems design (ISD) was described as a process used to analyze, design, develop, deliver, and evaluate training programs. Human resource development was described as a discipline meant to carry out the HPI process. Thus, the title HPI practitioner represents anyone who solves business problems using the HPI model.

Key Findings

The 1996 study found two key points. The first was that everyone in organizational settings plays a part in improving performance and contributes to enhanced organizational competitiveness. Practitioners, line managers, employees, and others may perform HPI work; HRD professionals are not its sole practitioners. The second point was that no individual plays all the roles or masters all the competencies described in the study.

In addition, the report:

- Listed trends in five areas: performance, business, learning, organizational structure, and technology.
- Described 14 terminal outputs of HPI work and 81 enabling outputs. A terminal output was described as a final outcome directly associated with a particular role, while an enabling output was described as a specific output associated with the demonstration of a particular competency.
- Pinpointed 15 core and 38 supporting competencies of HPI.
- Summarized four roles of HPI professionals: analyst, intervention specialist, change manager, and evaluator.
- Identified 16 key ethical issues affecting HPI work.

1989
Models for HRD Practice

The *Models for HRD Practice* report defined the profession to include career development and organization development as well as training and development. It defined HRD as "the integrated use of training and development, organization development, and career development to improve individual, group, and organizational effectiveness."

Key Findings

The 1989 study depicted HRD within the larger human resource field as a wheel encompassing 12 activities including training and development, organization development, career development, organization/job design, human resource planning, performance management systems, selection and staffing, compensation and benefits, employee assistance, union/labor relations, human resource research, and information systems.

In addition, the study:

- described 74 outputs of HRD work and identified quality requirements for each output
- pinpointed 35 competencies for HRD and identified key ethical issues affecting HRD
- summarized 11 HRD roles, including researcher, marketer, organization change agent, needs analyst, program designer, HRD materials developer, instructor/facilitator, individual career development advisor, administrator, evaluator, and HRD manager.

1983
Models for Excellence

The *Models for Excellence* report defined training and development and established the format for every ASTD Competency Model study published after 1983.

Key Findings

Models for Excellence was launched in 1981 when Patricia McLagan carried out a series of studies focused on training and development and the trainer's role. The 1983 report (McLagan and McCullough 1983) included a depiction of HRD as a wheel, a definition of training and development, a list of 34 forces expected to affect the T&D field, 15 T&D roles, 102 critical outputs for the T&D field, 31 T&D competencies, four role clusters, and a matrix of 15 roles and 31 competencies.

1978
A Study of Professional Training and Development Roles and Competencies

A Study of Professional Training and Development Roles and Competencies defined the basic skills, knowledge, and other attributes required for effective performance of training and development activities. The study questioned more than 14,000

ASTD members in the United States, Canada, and Mexico, and 500 members outside North America.

Key Findings

The 1978 study, conducted by Patrick Pinto and James Walker, revealed the following major areas for T&D practitioners:

- analyzing and diagnosing needs
- determining appropriate training approaches
- designing and developing programs
- developing material resources
- managing internal resources
- managing external resources
- developing and counseling individuals
- preparing job- or performance-related training
- conducting classroom training
- developing group and organization development
- conducting research on training
- managing working relationships with managers and clients
- managing the training and development function
- managing professional self-development.

Appendix C
Data Collection Details

The 2019 ATD Competency Study is a comprehensive and rigorous research project designed to identify the knowledge, skills, and abilities (KSAs) that are needed for effective performance as a talent development professional today and five years into the future. The 2019 Capability Model was developed using the data from that research and several other sources:

- a literature review of books, periodicals, research reports, and academic journal articles
- structured interviews with 25 thought leaders
- an occupational survey of talent development professionals.

Literature Review

The purpose of the literature review was to compile a broad base of information about talent development and analyze the information to identify thematic clusters that could be collapsed into statements that describe specific competencies. For this study, ATD adopted a definition of competency that integrated a variety of perspectives on the purpose of competencies and competency models for whole occupations, rather than a single job within an occupation. This approach required that the competencies generalize across jobs and regions of the world and, as such, excluded the use of job-specific behaviors (such as tasks and duties) or personal attributes that tend to vary across cultures (such as attitudes and values). As a result, ATD defined a competency as a statement describing knowledge or skills that are related to successful performance at work. Consistent with best practices in competency modeling, ATD focused on competencies that are linked to individual and organizational outcomes within the talent development profession.

The research resulted in information that either confirmed existing competencies related to talent development or described knowledge and skills that might be useful in the future. These data were then used to develop draft statements for review by subject matter experts for inclusion on the occupational survey.

Structured Interviews

ATD developed a structured interview questionnaire to gather perspectives about the scope and nature of talent development from experts and thought leaders currently working in or affiliated with the field. The questionnaire covered four main topics: defining talent development, the future of talent development, contributions to individual and organizational outcomes, and the 2013 ATD Competency Model. The entire questionnaire included 31 questions.

ATD staff administered the questionnaire to 25 experts and thought leaders either via a live virtual interview, when possible, or a written document. A summary of the interview insights follows.

Defining Talent Development

- Talent development is a holistic system of activities—ranging from acquisition to retention—that focus on the relationship between individual and organizational performance, capacity, and growth.
- Talent development is planned, theory driven, and outcome oriented, and it employs a mixed strategic and tactical orientation to achieve immediate and long-term goals.
- Talent development professionals include mid-career and higher professionals coming from other industries and departments (such as former business, HR, finance, healthcare, manufacturing, and education professionals) as well as early career professionals who may be more educated but less experienced (such as new graduates with degrees in HR, MBA, L&D, psychology, or education).
- Talent development professionals may specialize in a particular area such as coaching, or they may generalize across many areas of expertise including project management, organization development, quality assurance,

change management, data analytics, consulting, coaching, performance measurement, leadership, engagement, corporate responsibility, succession planning, onboarding, forecasting, and diversity and inclusion.

The Future of Talent Development

- The talent development profession is adapting to disruptions in the global marketplace. Talent is in short supply and demand is increasing. Speed, expectations, and complexity of work are increasing. People are staying at organizations for fewer years and may be looking at positions as stepping stones rather than careers. Meanwhile, organizations are reshaping in response to changing business models and emerging technology. Technology may be driving and enabling changes to occur in how work is done, what employees expect from their employers, and how organizations achieve competitive advantage.

- Talent development professionals increasingly need to enhance their ability to communicate how talent development contributes to organizations, develop a greater focus on strategic planning, enhance their ability to show measurable behavior change, experiment and deploy new models of talent development, partner with business leaders and stakeholders to understand the core business and the organization's strategic and operational environment, speak the language of business, develop the ability to discern the quality of talent development technologies, and identify current and future trends and their impact on the talent strategy.

Contributions to Individual and Organizational Outcomes

- Talent development contributes to the following individual outcomes: employee engagement and well-being, performance improvement, development of job-related competencies, career planning, compliance, customer service, product knowledge, interpersonal skills, and self-efficacy.

- Talent development contributes to the following organizational outcomes: onboarding, succession planning, profitability, customer experience and satisfaction, risk mitigation and compliance, operational effectiveness, knowledge sharing, culture and diversity, and retention.

The 2013 ATD Competency Model

In general, feedback about the 2013 model suggest that it is comprehensive, but perhaps a little outdated in terms of terminology and organized around the old way of thinking about the purpose and scope of talent development. It is unclear how the model components work together (for example, is one competency more or less important than another, and if so, under what circumstances?).

The model may only be meaningful to talent development professionals, thus limiting is applicability and frequency of adoption by the general public. The model needs to focus less on traditional training and learning models and include more information on how the AOEs impact the business. The model should emphasize that talent development is part of the business, not a separate entity.

The Occupational Survey of TD Professionals

Using drafted statements resulting from data obtained during the literature review, combined with trends identified through the structured interviews, subject matter experts reviewed, edited, and developed a total of 197 knowledge and skill statements to distribute as part of an occupational survey referred to as the "competency study." Given the length of the survey, which also included demographic questions, the survey was divided into three forms, each containing approximately 65 statements. To ensure equal distribution of the three survey forms, each respondent was randomly assigned an instrument. All demographic questions were the same.

The survey was distributed directly to ATD stakeholders via email, as well as through an open link across a variety of professional networks. Recipients of the survey were encouraged to share the link with talent development colleagues.

A total of 5,403 individuals accessed the survey. Of those, responses from 3,033 were determined to be valid. A valid response was identified as a survey that had at least 56 percent of the questions completed. In addition, respondents who gave the same rating for 90 percent or more of the survey were also excluded from analysis. Valid responses came from all three forms of the survey in near equal proportion, with Form A getting 1, 026 (19.0 percent) valid responses, Form B recording 1,049 (19.4 percent) valid responses, and Form C totaling 958 (17.7 percent) valid responses.

Because the list of statements included knowledge *and* skills, and the potential respondent group included individuals from across the career level spectrum (entry-level to executive), it was determined that traditional competency modeling scales assessing frequency, proficiency, and needed at entry represented an ill-fit for the focus of the study and would be difficult for some respondents to use. Instead, the study used a four-point importance scale to assess the importance of the listed knowledge and skills at two time points. For each statement, respondents rated the importance of the knowledge or skill for successful job performance today and in three to five years. The rating scales are shown below.

How important is this knowledge or skill for you to perform your job successfully today?
1-Not important
2-Minimally important
3-Moderately Important
4-Very important

How important will this knowledge or skill be for you to perform your job successfully in 3 to 5 years?
1-Not important
2-Minimally important
3-Moderately Important
4-Very important

Survey Results

In total, 188 knowledge and skill statements received a high enough average rating to be included in the 2019 Capability Model. Six KSA statements did not receive ratings high enough to be included, and an additional four statements were identified as duplicate content and removed for clarity.

The following tables, which are grouped by domain, break down the statistics for each capability's KSA statement. Each statement was rated on a four-point scale, with one being least important and four being most important. In addition to the number of respondents, the tables show the mean and standard deviation for each statement's ratings for both today and three to five years in the future.

Developing Personal Capability

Communication					
Statement	N	Mean Current	SD Current	Mean Future	SD Future
Skill in expressing thoughts, feelings, and ideas in a clear, concise, and compelling manner.	836	3.55	0.73	3.67	0.65
Skill in applying principles of active listening (for example, focusing on what someone is saying, deferring judgment, and responding appropriately).	796	3.62	0.62	3.70	0.56
Skill in using communication strategies that inform and influence audiences.	780	3.44	0.76	3.61	0.67
Skill in applying persuasion and influencing techniques to gain agreement, commitment, and buy-in from stakeholders.	882	3.32	0.83	3.48	0.76
Skill in conceiving, developing, and delivering information in various formats and media (for example reports, briefings, memorandums, presentations, articles, and emails).	796	3.37	0.77	3.51	0.70
Skill in applying verbal, written, and nonverbal communication techniques (for example, agenda setting, asking open-ended questions, use of posture and deference, and demonstrating professional presence).	796	3.51	0.73	3.60	0.67
Skill in facilitating dialogue with individuals and groups to help them identify, articulate, and clarify their thoughts and feelings.	780	3.20	0.89	3.39	0.80
Skill in articulating and conveying value propositions to gain agreement, support, and buy-in from stakeholders.	882	3.34	0.82	3.54	0.74

Each statement was rated on a scale of 1-4, where 1 = not important and 4 = very important.

Emotional Intelligence & Decision Making					
Statement	N	Mean Current	SD Current	Mean Future	SD Future
Knowledge of theories of emotional intelligence.	1,026	3.15	0.82	3.37	0.77
Skill in assessing and managing one's own emotional state.	776	3.31	0.90	3.44	0.84
Skill in identifying personal biases that influence one's own cognition and behavior.	776	3.30	0.88	3.45	0.79
Skill in observing and interpreting the verbal and nonverbal behavior of individuals and groups.	773	3.37	0.79	3.48	0.73
Skill in adjusting their own behavior in response to or anticipation of changes in others' behavior, attitudes, and thoughts.	776	3.40·	0.81	3.53	0.75
Knowledge of techniques and approaches to learn and demonstrate resilience (for example, meditation, mindfulness, and perspective-taking).	776	3.04	0.97	3.24	0.92
Knowledge of decision-making models (for example, consensus-based, democratic, and autocratic).	923	2.62	0.99	2.81	0.97
Skill in using logic and reasoning to identify the strengths and weaknesses of alternative solutions, conclusions, or approaches to problems.	776	3.42	0.76	3.54	0.71

Each statement was rated on a scale of 1-4, where 1 = not important and 4 = very important.

Collaboration & Leadership					
Statement	N	Mean Current	SD Current	Mean Future	SD Future
Knowledge of theories, methods, and techniques to build and manage professional relationships (for example, group dynamics, teamwork, shared experience, and negotiation).	816	3.11	0.84	3.31	0.80
Knowledge of methods and criteria for establishing and managing collaboration among various units (for example, finance, operations, IT, and sales and marketing).	816	2.88	0.93	3.14	0.90
Skill in building and managing teams and work groups (for example, leveraging group dynamics and fostering teamwork and collaboration).	816	3.28	0.83	3.53	0.72
Skill in integrating and synthesizing others' viewpoints to build alignment of diverse perspectives.	816	3.15	0.86	3.39	0.79
Knowledge of conflict management techniques.	923	3.04	0.90	3.23	0.83
Skill in managing conflict (for example, providing feedback and mediating and resolving disputes).	923	3.06	0.92	3.27	0.84
Knowledge of methods and techniques for managing and supervising others (for example, directing others' work, delegating tasks, providing guidance and support, and allocating tools and resources).	923	3.03	0.94	3.29	0.88
Knowledge of principles and techniques for providing feedback	796	3.38	0.77	3.56	0.68
Knowledge of leadership theories (for example, transformational, inclusive, and situational).	923	2.83	0.94	3.09	0.91
Skill in matching, assigning, and delegating work to others.	923	2.88	0.93	3.12	0.90

Each statement was rated on a scale of 1-4, where 1 = not important and 4 = very important.

Culture Awareness and Inclusion					
Statement	N	Mean Current	SD Current	Mean Future	SD Future
Knowledge of cultural differences in the workplace (for example, styles of communication, organizational and business customs, attire, and family obligations).	836	3.03	0.89	3.29	0.85
Knowledge of social and cultural norms that influence decision making and behavior.	836	2.92	0.92	3.17	0.87
Knowledge of methods and techniques to foster cultural awareness, encourage cultural sensitivity, and broaden viewpoints.	836	2.90	0.95	3.21	0.88
Skill in adapting and adjusting attitude, perspective, and behavior to function effectively in diverse environments or situations.	776	3.41	0.80	3.54	0.74
Knowledge of approaches to encourage and promote workplace diversity and inclusion.	836	2.87	0.97	3.16	0.92
Skill in integrating diversity and inclusion principles in talent development strategies and initiatives.	836	2.93	0.95	3.27	0.90

Each statement was rated on a scale of 1-4, where 1 = not important and 4 = very important.

Project Management					
Statement	N	Mean Current	SD Current	Mean Future	SD Future
Knowledge of project management principles and processes (for example, scheduling, planning, allocating resources, evaluating, and reporting).	976	3.10	0.85	3.31	0.81
Skill in coordinating the logistical tasks associated with planning meetings.	864	2.82	0.96	2.82	0.98
Skill in evaluating and prioritizing implications, risks, feasibility, and consequences of potential activities.	774	3.16	0.89	3.33	0.82
Skill in developing project plans and schedules that integrate resources, tasks, and timelines.	976	3.07	0.86	3.26	0.85
Skill in adjusting work processes and outputs in response to or anticipation of changes in goals, standards, resources, and time.	923	3.04	0.97	3.28	0.81
Skill in establishing, monitoring, and communicating progress toward the achievement of goals, objectives, and milestones.	976	3.24	0.81	3.47	0.75

Each statement was rated on a scale of 1-4, where 1 = not important and 4 = very important.

Compliance and Ethical Behavior					
Statement	N	Mean Current	SD Current	Mean Future	SD Future
Skill in acting with integrity (for example, being honest, acknowledging own mistakes, and treating people with dignity, respect, and fairness).	773	3.71	0.63	3.76	0.58
Skill in establishing, maintaining, and enforcing standards for integrity and ethical behavior in self and others.	923	3.13	0.95	3.28	0.90
Knowledge of laws, regulations, and ethical issues related to the access and use of information (for example, intellectual capital, personally identifiable information, and customer data).	930	2.99	0.95	3.22	0.91
Knowledge of laws, regulations, and ethical issues related to the development of instructional content (for example, intellectual property and copyright laws and accessibility requirements).	1,026	3.02	0.90	3.19	0.90
Knowledge of laws, regulations, and ethical issues related to human resources and talent development (for example, employment law, accessibility, and labor relations).	1,026	2.84	0.96	3.04	0.94
Knowledge of laws, regulations, and ethical issues related to the employment of permanent, contingent, and dispersed workforces.	930	2.55	0.99	2.79	1.02
Knowledge of region- or market-specific education and labor public policies.	929	2.41	0.99	2.59	1.01

Each statement was rated on a scale of 1-4, where 1 = not important and 4 = very important.

Lifelong Learning					
Statement	N	Mean Current	SD Current	Mean Future	SD Future
Knowledge of how a desire to learn can lead to the expansion and development of knowledge and skills over time.	1,026	3.15	0.83	3.28	0.81
Skill in acquiring new knowledge through professional development activities for one's self (for example, attending professional conferences, self-directed reading, and monitoring industry trends).	773	3.51	0.74	3.65	0.63
Skill in developing, maintaining, and leveraging networks across a range of people and groups inside and outside the organization (for example, influential people and learning and performance experts).	816	3.16	0.88	3.43	0.79
Knowledge of resources for career exploration and lifelong learning for self and others.	845	2.84	0.95	3.15	0.91

Each statement was rated on a scale of 1-4, where 1 = not important and 4 = very important.

Building Professional Capability

Learning Sciences					
Statement	N	Mean Current	SD Current	Mean Future	SD Future
Knowledge of the foundational learning theories of behaviorism, cognitivism, and constructivism.	1,026	2.79	0.88	2.82	0.92
Knowledge of the principles and applications of cognitive science for learning (for example auditory and visual processing, information storage and retrieval, memory, and cognitive load).	1,026	3.18	0.80	3.31	0.79
Knowledge of adult learning theories and models (for example, Knowles' Adult Learning Theory, Bloom's Taxonomy, Gagne's Nine Levels of Learning, Mager's Criterion-Referenced Instruction Approach, social and collaborative learning, and experiential learning).	1,026	3.31	0.81	3.28	0.84
Knowledge of communication theories and models and how they relate to learning.	836	2.59	1.01	2.81	0.97
Skill in applying principles of cognitive science and adult learning to design solutions that maximize learning and behavioral outcomes (for example, enhancing motivation and increasing knowledge retention).	1,026	3.40	0.74	3.54	0.69

Each statement was rated on a scale of 1-4, where 1 = not important and 4 = very important.

Instructional Design					
Statement	N	Mean Current	SD Current	Mean Future	SD Future
Skill in developing learning and behavioral outcome statements.	881	3.17	0.84	3.36	0.79
Knowledge of instructional design models and processes (for example, ADDIE and SAM).	881	3.10	0.91	3.15	0.91
Knowledge of needs assessment approaches and techniques.	881	3.31	0.78	3.48	0.69
Knowledge of instructional modalities (for example, classroom learning, blended learning, massive open online courses or MOOCs, gamification, multi-device and mobile learning, and virtual reality simulations).	881	3.31	0.81	3.54	0.70
Knowledge of methods and techniques for defining learning and behavioral outcome statements.	881	3.21	0.84	3.36	0.79
Knowledge of the criteria used to assess the quality and relevance of instructional content in relation to a desired learning or behavioral outcome.	845	3.12	0.88	3.37	0.80
Skill in designing blueprints, schematics, and other visual representations of learning and development solutions (for example, wireframes, storyboards, and mock-ups).	864	2.67	0.98	2.92	0.95
Knowledge of methods and techniques for planning, designing, and developing instructional content.	881	3.36	0.78	3.44	0.76
Skill in eliciting and using knowledge and information from subject matter experts to support and enhance learning.	816	3.40	0.76	3.56	0.69
Knowledge of types and applications of instructional methods and techniques (for example, discussion, self-directed learning, role playing, lecture, action learning, demonstration, and exercise).	881	3.41	0.79	3.51	0.71
Skill in selecting and aligning delivery options and media for training and learning events to the desired learning or behavioral outcomes.	864	3.30	0.82	3.50	0.76
Skill in designing and developing learning assets (for example, role plays, self-assessments, training manuals, job aids, and visual aids) that align to a desired learning or behavioral outcome.	864	3.26	0.84	3.37	0.81
Knowledge of how design thinking and rapid prototyping can be applied to the development of learning and talent development solutions.	845	2.76	0.91	3.20	0.88
Knowledge of how formal and informal learning experiences influence and support individual and group development.	838	3.22	0.78	3.48	0.68

Each statement was rated on a scale of 1-4, where 1 = not important and 4 = very important.

Training Delivery and Facilitation					
Statement	N	Mean Current	SD Current	Mean Future	SD Future
Skill in coordinating the logistical tasks associated with planning meetings or learning events.	864	2.82	0.96	2.82	0.98
Skill in facilitating meetings or learning events in face-to-face and virtual environments.	864	3.25	0.85	3.34	0.83
Knowledge of facilitation methods and techniques.	864	3.36	0.81	3.40	0.80
Skill in creating positive learning climates and environments.	864	3.51	0.76	3.60	0.71
Skill in selecting and aligning delivery options and media for training and learning events to the desired learning or behavioral outcomes.	864	3.30	0.82	3.50	0.76

Training Delivery and Facilitation (cont.)					
Statement	N	Mean Current	SD Current	Mean Future	SD Future
Skill in delivering training using multiple delivery options and media (for example, mobile or multi-device, online, classroom, or multimedia).	864	3.23	0.87	3.50	0.77
Skill in designing and developing learning assets (for example, role plays, self-assessments, training manuals, job aids, and visual aids) that align to a desired learning or behavioral outcome.	864	3.26	0.84	3.37	0.81

Each statement was rated on a scale of 1-4, where 1 = not important and 4 = very important.

Technology Application					
Statement	N	Mean Current	SD Current	Mean Future	SD Future
Skill in selecting, integrating, managing, and maintaining learning platforms (for example, learning management systems, knowledge management systems, and performance management systems).	780	2.89	1.00	3.17	0.92
Skill identifying, defining, and articulating technology system requirements to support learning and talent development solutions.	776	2.81	0.96	3.08	0.90
Knowledge of criteria and techniques for evaluating and selecting e-learning software and tools.	780	2.82	0.97	3.10	0.91
Skill in identifying, selecting, and implementing learning technologies (for example, using evaluative criteria and identifying appropriate applications in an instructional environment).	776	2.95	0.94	3.20	0.87
Knowledge of methods and techniques for testing the usability and functionality of learning technologies and support systems.	780	2.70	0.96	2.99	0.95
Knowledge of existing learning technologies and support systems (for example, collaborative learning software, learning management systems, authoring tools, and social media).	780	3.17	0.83	3.53	0.69
Knowledge of human resources systems and technology platforms and how they integrate with other organizational and business systems and processes.	780	2.66	0.98	2.95	0.96
Knowledge of communication technologies and their applications (for example, video conferencing, web conferencing, audience response systems, and presentation software).	780	3.17	0.83	3.42	0.78
Knowledge of principles of user interface design.	780	2.67	0.97	3.00	0.96
Skill in developing artificial intelligence, machine learning algorithms, augmented reality, and mixed reality that are ethical and free of bias.	792	1.98	1.04	2.53	1.16
Skill in using e-learning software and tools.	776	3.02	0.96	3.28	0.90
Knowledge of functions, features, limitations, and practical applications of the technologies available to support learning and talent development solutions.	780	3.11	0.83	3.41	0.76
Skill in using human resource technology systems to store, retrieve, and process talent and talent development-related information.	883	2.64	1.01	2.99	1.00
Knowledge of techniques and approaches to leverage social media platforms and tools to support knowledge sharing, idea exchange, and learning.	838	2.78	0.95	3.31	0.85
Knowledge of artificial intelligence, machine learning algorithms, augmented reality, and mixed reality that are ethical and free of bias.	792	1.98	1.04	2.53	1.16

Each statement was rated on a scale of 1-4, where 1 = not important and 4 = very important.

Knowledge Management					
Statement	**N**	**Mean Current**	**SD Current**	**Mean Future**	**SD Future**
Knowledge of principles of knowledge management (for example, conceptualizing, managing, preserving, or maintaining organizational knowledge).	882	2.96	0.87	3.23	0.83
Knowledge of methods and techniques for capturing and codifying knowledge (for example, storytelling, data mining, cognitive mapping, decision trees, or knowledge taxonomies).	882	2.82	0.92	3.17	0.89
Knowledge of methods and techniques for disseminating or sharing knowledge across individuals, groups, and organizations.	838	3.10	0.84	3.40	0.78
Skill in designing and implementing knowledge management strategy.	1,049	2.87	0.92	3.22	0.85
Skill in identifying the quality, authenticity, accuracy, impartiality, or relevance of information from various sources (for example, databases, print and online media, speeches and presentations, and observations).	838	2.98	0.96	3.23	0.91
Skill in curating instructional content, tools, and resources (for example, researching, evaluating, selecting, or assembling publicly available online courseware).	838	3.00	0.94	3.31	0.88
Skill in organizing and synthesizing information from multiple sources (for example, databases, print and online media, speeches and presentations, and observations).	816	2.97	0.91	3.19	0.89
Skill in identifying the type and amount of information needed to support talent development activities.	838	3.03	0.91	3.25	0.85
Skill in developing, managing, facilitating, or supporting knowledge networks and communities of practice.	837	2.93	0.91	3.31	0.79

Each statement was rated on a scale of 1-4, where 1 = not important and 4 = very important.

Career and Leadership Development					
Statement	**N**	**Mean Current**	**SD Current**	**Mean Future**	**SD Future**
Knowledge of how to develop and implement qualification programs.	910	2.48	1.01	2.76	1.02
Skill in developing, administering, and debriefing the results of assessments of intelligence, aptitude, potential, skill, ability, or interests.	792	2.84	1.00	3.15	0.93
Skill in facilitating the career development planning process (for example, helping employees identify needs and career goals and preparing development plans).	845	2.62	1.03	3.00	1.02
Knowledge of career development methods and techniques (for example, job rotations and stretch assignments).	845	2.65	0.99	3.01	0.99
Skill in conducting individual and group career planning sessions to provide guidance across career phases (for example, onboarding and job changes).	845	2.44	1.05	2.80	1.03
Knowledge of career models and paths (such as vertical, horizontal, project-based, and matrix).	845	2.41	0.99	2.79	0.99
Knowledge of leadership development practices and techniques (for example, formal training programs, job rotation, and coaching or mentoring).	845	3.04	0.92	3.35	0.82
Skill in sourcing, designing, building, and evaluating leadership development experiences.	958	3.01	0.96	3.33	0.88

Each statement was rated on a scale of 1-4, where 1 = not important and 4 = very important.

Coaching					
Statement	N	Mean Current	SD Current	Mean Future	SD Future
Knowledge of organizational coaching models.	845	2.57	1.03	2.95	0.99
Skill in helping individuals or teams identify goals, develop realistic action plans, seek development opportunities, and monitor progress and accountability.	958	3.34	0.85	3.51	0.74
Skill in coaching supervisors and managers on methods and approaches for supporting employee development.	958	3.18	0.95	3.45	0.81
Skill in creating effective coaching agreements.	838	2.43	1.05	2.80	1.03
Knowledge of methods and techniques to evaluate the effectiveness of coaching.	838	2.77	0.99	3.17	0.91
Skill in establishing an environment that fosters mutual respect and trust with coaching clients.	838	2.79	1.09	3.12	1.01
Skill in recruiting, training, and pairing coaches or mentors with employees.	838	2.55	1.03	2.96	1.02
Knowledge of professional standards and ethical guidelines for coaching.	838	2.84	1.02	3.14	0.94

Each statement was rated on a scale of 1-4, where 1 = not important and 4 = very important.

Evaluating Impact					
Statement	N	Mean Current	SD Current	Mean Future	SD Future
Knowledge of models and methods to evaluate the impact of learning and talent development solutions.	798	3.12	0.86	3.46	0.75
Knowledge of qualitative and quantitative data collection methods, techniques, and tools (for example, observations, interviews, focus groups, surveys, or assessments).	798	2.78	0.93	3.10	0.89
Skill in creating data collection tools (for example, questionnaires, surveys, and structured interviews).	798	2.97	0.92	3.22	0.85
Knowledge of research design methodologies and types (for example, experimental, correlational, descriptive, meta-analytic, longitudinal, and cross-sectional).	798	2.29	0.98	2.60	1.01
Skill in selecting or designing organizational research (for example, defining research questions, creating hypotheses, and selecting methodologies).	798	2.32	1.03	2.66	1.03
Skill in identifying and defining individual or organizational outcome metrics based on the evaluation strategy or business objectives of a solution.	798	2.92	0.95	3.24	0.89

Each statement was rated on a scale of 1-4, where 1 = not important and 4 = very important.

Impacting Organizational Capability

Business Insight					
Statement	N	Mean Current	SD Current	Mean Future	SD Future
Knowledge of business or organizational processes, operations, and outputs (for example, governance structures, business models, products, and services).	989	2.06	0.90	3.23	0.87
Knowledge of business strategies and factors that influence an organization's competitive position in the industry.	929	3.10	0.90	3.33	0.83
Knowledge of how organizations provide customer service (for example, anticipating and assessing needs, meeting quality standards for services, and evaluating customer satisfaction).	929	3.24	0.87	3.43	0.82
Knowledge of how talent development contributes to an organization's competitive advantage.	929	3.20	0.91	3.43	0.82
Knowledge of financial management principles (for example, pricing, contracts, budgeting, accounting, forecasting, and reporting).	929	2.59	0.95	2.85	0.96
Skill in managing budgets and resources.	882	2.81	0.96	3.15	0.89
Skill in creating business cases for talent development initiatives using economic, financial, and organizational data.	882	2.93	0.94	3.31	0.87
Skill in communicating business and financial information to different audiences using the appropriate terminology and relevant examples.	796	2.90	0.99	3.18	0.92

Each statement was rated on a scale of 1-4, where 1 = not important and 4 = very important.

Consulting and Business Partnering					
Statement	N	Mean Current	SD Current	Mean Future	SD Future
Skill in establishing and managing organizational or business partnerships and relationships.	816	3.28	0.84	3.49	0.73
Skill in partnering with other organizational units to provide guidance on departmental or organizational talent requirements.	816	3.06	0.92	3.31	0.87
Skill in managing stakeholders on an ongoing basis to sustain organizational or business relationships.	798	3.18	0.90	3.42	0.78
Knowledge of needs assessment approaches and techniques.	881	3.31	0.78	3.48	0.69
Skill in synthesizing information to formulate recommendations or a course of action to gain agreement, support, or buy-in from stakeholders.	882	3.26	0.82	3.46	0.76
Skill in conveying recommendations or a course of action to gain agreement, support, or buy-in from stakeholders.	882	3.33	0.81	3.50	0.73
Knowledge of methods and criteria for sourcing, establishing, or managing partnerships (for example, vendors, clients, suppliers, universities, and membership associations).	816	2.60	0.96	2.82	0.94
Skill in identifying, minimizing, and overcoming organizational barriers to implementing talent development solutions or strategies.	976	3.10	0.89	3.33	0.83

Each statement was rated on a scale of 1-4, where 1 = not important and 4 = very important.

Organization Development and Culture					
Statement	N	Mean Current	SD Current	Mean Future	SD Future
Knowledge of organization development concepts (for example, organizational design, job design, team formation, cultural norms, and culture transformation).	958	3.02	0.92	3.28	0.86
Skill in designing and implementing organization development strategy.	1,049	3.00	0.93	3.33	0.85
Knowledge of the theories and frameworks related to the design, interaction, and operation of social, organizational, and informational systems (for example, systems thinking, open systems theory, chaos and complexity theory, network theory, and action research).	1,026	2.77	0.91	3.02	0.91
Skill in identifying formal and informal relationships, hierarchies, and power dynamics in an organization.	881	2.82	0.96	2.98	0.94
Knowledge of the principles of organizational management (for example, division of labor, authority and responsibility, equity, order, and unity).	1,049	2.77	0.97	2.92	0.96
Knowledge of work roles, relationships, and reporting structures within an organization.	958	3.09	0.85	3.14	0.88
Knowledge of strategies and techniques for building, supporting, or promoting an organizational culture that values talent and learning as drivers of competitive advantage.	976	3.04	0.92	3.39	0.84
Skill in creating a culture which encourages and creates opportunities for dialogue and feedback between individuals and groups (for example, designing collaborative work practices and spaces, and role-modeling effective feedback techniques).	796	3.27	0.86	3.51	0.86
Skill in articulating and codifying talent and leadership principles, values, and competencies that guide the organization's culture and define behavioral expectations.	923	2.86	0.97	3.17	0.92
Knowledge of how employee engagement and retention influence organizational outcomes.	958	3.07	0.90	3.36	0.81
Knowledge of the principles, policies, and practices associated with programs and initiatives designed for organizational well-being (such as silos, job environment, toxicity, goal setting, job stability, and autonomy).	958	2.54	1.00	2.77	0.99
Skill in assessing and evaluating employee engagement.	910	2.81	0.98	3.13	0.92
Skill in designing and implementing employee engagement strategy.	1,049	2.99	0.94	3.31	0.88

Each statement was rated on a scale of 1-4, where 1 = not important and 4 = very important.

Talent Strategy and Management					
Statement	N	Mean Current	SD Current	Mean Future	SD Future
Knowledge of talent management functions (for example, workforce planning, acquisition, employee development, performance management, and compensation and rewards).	1,049	2.98	0.96	3.23	0.91
Skill in creating and aligning the talent development vision and strategy with the organizational and business vision and strategy.	977	3.22	0.91	3.50	0.80
Skill in developing a talent strategy that aligns to the organizational strategy to influence organizational outcomes in a positive direction.	976	3.17	0.94	3.46	0.83
Skill in designing and implementing strategic plans for talent development projects, programs, or functions.	976	3.06	0.92	3.34	0.84
Skill in identifying anticipated constraints or problems affecting talent development initiatives (for example, resource deficiencies or lack of support).	1,049	2.99	0.94	3.31	0.88
Skill in establishing and executing a marketing strategy to promote talent development.	1,049	2.63	1.02	3.00	1.01
Skill in designing and implementing communication strategy in order to drive talent management objectives.	1,049	3.16	0.84	3.39	0.77
Skill in communicating how talent development strategies and solutions support the achievement of targeted business and organizational results.	796	3.21	0.86	3.49	0.76
Skill in communicating the value of learning and professional development.	836	3.19	0.90	3.43	0.78
Knowledge of succession planning and talent review processes (for example, assessment, scenario planning, talent mobility, and critical roles identification).	958	2.65	1.02	3.04	0.99
Knowledge of methods to identify the critical requirements of tasks, jobs, and roles (for example, job analysis, competency modeling, and leadership competency development).	958	3.16	0.87	3.36	0.79
Knowledge of talent acquisition strategies and concepts (for example, talent mobility, employment branding, sourcing, passive and active recruiting, and onboarding).	1,049	2.56	1.02	2.87	1.00
Skill in comparing and evaluating the advantages and disadvantages of talent development strategies (for example, developing internal employees versus hiring external talent).	976	2.65	1.02	2.98	0.98
Skill in developing workforce plans that articulate current and future talent and skill requirements.	923	2.84	0.96	3.20	0.90
Skill in designing and implementing a performance management strategy.	1,049	2.91	0.92	3.17	0.89
Knowledge of approaches for identifying and developing high potential talent.	845	2.76	1.02	3.15	0.98

Each statement was rated on a scale of 1-4, where 1 = not important and 4 = very important.

Performance Improvement					
Statement	N	Mean Current	SD Current	Mean Future	SD Future
Knowledge of the theories, models, and principles of human performance improvement.	910	2.88	0.91	3.15	0.88
Knowledge of performance analysis methods and techniques (for example, business process analysis, performance gap assessment, and root-cause analysis).	910	2.98	0.94	3.28	0.85
Knowledge of how human interactions with work environments, tools, equipment, and technology affect individual and organizational performance.	1,026	3.28	0.78	3.53	0.72
Skill in conducting a performance analysis to identify goals, gaps, or opportunities.	910	3.10	0.91	3.38	0.79
Skill in designing and developing performance improvement solutions to address performance gaps.	836	3.17	0.87	3.41	0.78
Skill in designing and implementing performance support systems and tools (for example, instructional resources, data, process models, job aids, and expert advice).	910	3.20	0.88	3.43	0.80
Skill in conducting an analysis of systems to improve human performance (for example, determining how organizations learn, closing knowledge or skills gaps, and addressing human factor issues).	836	3.00	0.92	3.32	0.83

Each statement was rated on a scale of 1-4, where 1 = not important and 4 = very important.

Change Management					
Statement	N	Mean Current	SD Current	Mean Future	SD Future
Knowledge of change management theories and models (for example, Lewin, Kotter, Bridges' transition model, Kubler-Ross change curve, and appreciative inquiry).	910	2.60	0.99	2.95	0.94
Knowledge of how change impacts people and organizations.	910	3.15	0.87	3.41	0.77
Skill in assessing risk, resistance, and consequences to define a change management approach.	910	2.83	0.96	3.1	0.88
Skill in designing and implementing an organizational change strategy.	1,049	2.98	0.91	3.36	0.82

Each statement was rated on a scale of 1-4, where 1 = not important and 4 = very important.

Data and Analytics					
Statement	**N**	**Mean Current**	**SD Current**	**Mean Future**	**SD Future**
Knowledge of the principles and applications of analytics (for example, big data, predictive modeling, data mining, machine learning, and business intelligence).	798	2.53	0.98	3.06	0.98
Skill in identifying stakeholders' needs, goals, requirements, questions, and objectives to develop a framework or plan for data analysis.	798	3.03	0.97	3.27	3.21
Skill in gathering and organizing data from internal or external sources in logical and practical ways to support retrieval and manipulation.	792	2.77	0.96	3.04	0.91
Skill in analyzing and interpreting the results of data analyses to identify patterns, trends, and relationships among variables.	792	2.91	0.96	3.21	0.89
Knowledge of data visualization, including principles, methods, types, and applications (for example, texture and color mapping, data representation, graphs, and word clouds).	796	2.60	0.98	2.94	0.95
Skill in selecting or using data visualization techniques (for example, flow charts, graphs, plots, word clouds, and heat maps).	796	2.74	0.93	3.04	0.92
Knowledge of statistical theory and methods, including the computation, interpretation, and reporting of statistics.	798	2.34	0.98	2.70	1.01

Each statement was rated on a scale of 1-4, where 1 = not important and 4 = very important.

Future Readiness					
Statement	**N**	**Mean Current**	**SD Current**	**Mean Future**	**SD Future**
Knowledge of internal and external factors that influence talent development (for example, organizational and business strategies, availability of labor, developments in other industries, societal trends, and technological advances).	929	3.06	0.91	3.30	0.86
Skill in conducting environmental scanning to identify current and emerging trends in the economy, legislation, competition, and technology.	929	2.56	0.99	2.86	1.01
Knowledge of techniques to promote, support, or generate innovation and creativity (for example, design thinking, brainstorming, and ideation).	773	3.44	0.72	3.64	0.62
Knowledge of emerging learning technologies and support systems (for example, collaborative learning software, learning management systems, authoring tools, and social media).	780	3.17	0.83	3.53	0.69
Knowledge of information-seeking strategies and techniques.	838	2.93	0.89	3.15	3.09
Skill in applying one's own previous learning to future experiences.	773	3.64	0.65	3.71	0.59

Each statement was rated on a scale of 1-4, where 1 = not important and 4 = very important.

Demographic Details

The 2019 ATD Capability Study was the largest of its kind to date, with 3,033 valid responses. The following tables outline the respondent demographics.

Respondent Age		
Age	Frequency	Percent
15 – 20 years	0	0
21 – 30 years	178	5.9
31 – 40 years	715	23.6
41 – 50 years	817	26.9
51 – 60 years	700	23.1
61 – 70 years	214	7.1
71 – 75	26	0.9
I prefer not to answer	367	12.1

Years of Professional Experience in Talent Development		
Years of Experience	Frequency	Percent
Less than 1 year	87	2.9
1 to 2 years	146	4.8
3 to 5 years	456	15.0
6 to 10 years	561	18.5
11 to 15 years	529	17.4
16 to 20 years	505	16.7
21 to 30 years	529	17.4
More than 30 years	220	7.3

Highest Level of Education Completed		
Educational Background	Frequency	Percent
Secondary education (e.g., high school, gymnasia, preparatory school) diploma, certificate, or equivalent	33	1.1
Trade/Vocational school diploma or certificate	27	0.9
Some college/university coursework	179	5.9
College/University degree (e.g. Associate's, Bachelor's, Baccalaureate) College/University degree (e.g. Associate's, Bachelor's, Baccalaureate) College/University degree (e.g. Associate's, Bachelor's, Baccalaureate)	1,073	35.4
Post-graduate (e.g. Master's, Doctorate)	1,670	55.1

Current Career Level		
Career Level	Frequency	Percent
Entry-Level	82	2.7
Mid-Level Specialist	541	17.8
Senior-Level Specialist	759	25.0
Entry-Level Manager	161	5.3
Mid-Level Manager	516	17.0
Senior-Level Manager	475	15.7
Executive	176	5.8
Senior Executive	112	3.7
CEO or Head of organization	211	7.0

Type of Employer Organization, Institution, or Business		
Organization Type	Frequency	Percent
Domestic for profit	1,009	33.3
Multinational for profit	976	32.2
Domestic not-for-profit	337	11.1
Government	268	8.8
Academic institution	202	6.7
Other	144	4.7
Multinational not-for-profit	79	2.6
Military	18	0.6

Size of Employer Organization, Institution, or Business		
Organization Size	Frequency	Percent
1	173	5.7
2-10	182	6.0
11-50	140	4.6
51-100	81	2.7
101-500	450	14.8
501-2,500	627	20.7
2,501-10,000	564	18.6
10,001-50,000	454	15.0
50,001-100,000	181	6.0
100,001 or more	160	5.3

Size of the Talent Development Function		
Number of People	Frequency	Percent
1	472	15.6
2-5	888	29.3
6-10	484	16.0
11-50	641	21.1
51-100	178	5.9
101-500	202	6.7
501-2,500	90	3.0
2,501-5,000	20	0.7
5,001 or more	24	0.8

Where the Talent Development Function Reports		
Department	Frequency	Percent
Human Resources	1,433	47.2
Operations	502	16.6
My organization is a small company/sole proprietorship/ talent development consultancy	380	12.5
CEO/Executive Office	362	11.9
Other	44	1.5
Finance	31	1.0

Primary Employer Sector		
Sector	Frequency	Percent
Professional Services (HR, Employment, Research, Consulting, Education/Training, Credentialing/Licensure)	618	20.4
Healthcare	314	10.4
Finance	280	9.2
Manufacturing	208	6.9
Academia	180	5.9
Information Technology Software	156	5.1
Insurance	148	4.9
Public Administration	112	3.7
Pharmaceuticals, Biotechnology & Life Sciences	109	3.6
Retail & Trade	107	3.5
Transportation & Warehousing	88	2.9
Hospitality & Food Service	82	2.7
Utilities	62	2.0
Military/National Defense	57	1.9
Oil & Gas	52	1.7
Telecommunications	47	1.5
Media, Arts & Entertainment	41	1.4
Real Estate	41	1.4
Information Technology Hardware & Equipment	39	1.3
Commercial Services (Printing, Facilities, Office Support, Security and Alarm)	27	0.9
Other	22	0.7
Agriculture, Fishing & Hunting	16	0.5
Social Services	15	0.5
Legal	12	0.4
Outsourcing	12	0.4
Mining & Forestry	9	0.3
International Development	9	0.3
Travel & Tourism	5	0.2
Library and Information Services	5	0.2

Country in Which Respondents Are Based					
Country	Frequency	Percent	Country	Frequency	Percent
United States	2,331	76.9	Iran	4	0.1
India	78	2.6	Qatar	4	0.1
Canada	54	1.8	Bangladesh	3	0.1
China	42	1.4	Belgium	3	0.1
Saudi Arabia	32	1.1	Denmark	3	0.1
Australia	24	0.8	France	3	0.1
Malaysia	24	0.8	Poland	3	0.1
Mexico	23	0.8	Spain	3	0.1
Singapore	18	0.6	Trinidad and Tobago	3	0.1
United Arab Emirates	18	0.6	Akrotiri	2	0.1
Egypt	17	0.6	Barbados	2	0.1
Nigeria	17	0.6	Cameroon	2	0.1
Philippines	17	0.6	Ethiopia	2	0.1
United Kingdom	17	0.6	Greece	2	0.1
Hong Kong	14	0.5	Ireland	2	0.1
South Africa	12	0.4	Liechtenstein	2	0.1
Brazil	11	0.4	New Zealand	2	0.1
Japan	11	0.4	Panama	2	0.1
Indonesia	10	0.3	Sweden	2	0.1
Pakistan	10	0.3	Uzbekistan	2	0.1
Germany	9	0.3	Aruba	1	0.0
Kenya	8	0.3	Austria	1	0.0
Turkey	8	0.3	Azerbaijan	1	0.0
Argentina	7	0.2	Belarus	1	0.0
Chile	7	0.2	Bermuda	1	0.0
Colombia	7	0.2	Bhutan	1	0.0
Korea, South	7	0.2	Botswana	1	0.0
Taiwan	7	0.2	Finland	1	0.0
Kuwait	6	0.2	Honduras	1	0.0
Puerto Rico	6	0.2	Macau	1	0.0
Bahamas, The	5	0.2	Macedonia	1	0.0
Bahrain	5	0.2	Morocco	1	0.0
Oman	5	0.2	Mozambique	1	0.0
Peru	5	0.2	Netherlands Antilles	1	0.0
Russia	5	0.2	Serbia and Montenegro	1	0.0
Switzerland	5	0.2	Sudan	1	0.0
Thailand	5	0.2			

Project Contributors

Competency Model Advisory Panel
- Britt Andreatta, CEO and President, Andreatta Consulting
- Elaine Biech, President, ebb associates inc.
- Nicole Carter, Talent Manager, US Venture Inc.
- John Coné, Principal, The Eleventh Hour Group
- Wendy Gates Corbett, CPLP, President, Refresher Training LLC
- David C. Forman, President, Sage Learning Systems
- Jonathan Halls, President and CEO, Jonathan Halls & Associates
- Karl Kapp, Professor and Consultant, Bloomsburg University, Institute for Interactive Technologies
- Dana Alan Koch, Global Learning Research and Innovation Lead, Accenture
- Jennifer Martineau, SVP Research, Evaluation & Societal Advancement, Center for Creative Leadership
- Pat McLagan, CEO, McLagan International Inc
- Kara Miller, Vice President, Comcast University, Comcast
- William Rothwell, President, Rothwell & Associates

With special thanks to Elaine Biech, John Coné, and William Rothwell for their guidance and support throughout the entirety of this project.

Competency Model Task Force
- Grace Amos, Senior Manager, Talent Enablement & Development, Cisco Meraki
- Jennifer Brink, Senior Director, L&D Talent Development, Comcast
- Brian Davis, CPLP, Learning & Development Division Manager, Washington Suburban Sanitary Commission
- Jessica Gil, Director, Manager Experience, Talent Management, European Wax Center
- Jennifer Halsall, Senior Manager, Talent Strategy, TD Bank
- Bahaa Hussein, CPLP, Managing Partner MENA, SIMDUSTRY
- John Kostek, Business Interlock Manager, Hitachi Ventara
- Lance Legree, Global Learning Business Partner, Hilti
- Jay Maxwell, CPLP, Business Operations and Training Consultant, Toyota Connected North America
- Kent Nuttall, CPLP, President, Torch Solutions Group
- Joseph Reamer, Academy Lead, HSBC Finance Corporation

Subject Matter Experts
- Michelle Baker, Talent Development Consultant, phase(two)learning
- Michelle Braden, Vice President, Global Learning and Talent Management, WEX Inc.
- Robert Brinkerhoff, Professor, Western Michigan University
- Brian Clouse, CPLP, Head, Corporate Learning Programs, Saudi Aramco
- JD Dillon, Chief Learning Architect, Axonify
- Diane Elkins, Artisan E-Learning
- Rodrigo Lara Fernandez, CEO, Mas Consultores

- Chuck Hodell, National Labor College
- Catherine Lombardozzi, Founder, Learning 4 Learning Professionals
- Seema Nagrath Menon, CPLP, Managing Director and Founder, Center for Action in Learning Management
- Jack Phillips, Chairman, ROI Institute
- Patti Phillips, CEO, ROI Institute
- Dave Ulrich, Co-Founder and Principal, RBL Group

ATD CTDO (Chief Talent Development Officer) Next Members
- Kimberly Currier, Senior Vice President, People Strategy, North Highland
- Tamar Elkeles, Chief Human Resources Officer, XCOM
- Tara Deakin, Chief Talent and Development Officer, Spin Master
- Suzanne Frawley, Director, Talent Management, Plains All American
- Joyce Gibson, Vice President, Instructional Design, Learning Technologies, and Technical Communications, Barclaycard US
- Regina Hartley, Vice President, Global Talent Management, UPS
- Jayne Johnson, Vice President, Enterprise Learning and Development, Alkermes
- Rebecca Jones, Chief People Officer, European Wax Center
- Kimo Kippen, President, Aloha Learning Advisors LLC; Former Chief Learning Officer, Hilton Hotels
- Brian Miller, Vice President, Talent, Development & Inclusion, Gilead Sciences
- Terri Pearce, Executive Vice President HR, Head, Learning and Talent Development, HSBC USA
- Eivind Slaaen, Head, People and Culture Development, Hilti Corporation
- Martha Soehren, Chief Talent Development Officer, Comcast
- Lou Tedrick, Vice President, Global Learning and Development, Verizon
- Tim Tobin, Vice President, Franchisee Onboarding and Learning, Choice Hotels
- Jim Woolsey, President, Defense Acquisition University

ATD National Advisors for Chapters (NAC)
- Chris Coladonato, CPLP, NAC Chair, Professional Development Leader, Farmers Insurance
- Elizabeth Beckham, Learning and Development Manager, Turner Industries Group LLC
- Roger Buskill, Faculty, University of Louisville
- Tracie Cantu, Director, Learning Technology, Whole Foods Market
- Krishna Clay, Senior Learning Advisor, HR, First National Bank of Omaha
- Bernadette Costello, Managing Partner, BCC Consulting LLC
- Lisa Goodpaster, Associate Director, Project Management, University of Illinois-Carle, Illinois College of Medicine
- David Hofstetter, Coach, Facilitator, Speaker, The Hofstetter Group
- Stephanie Hubka, CPLP, Managing Partner, Protos Learning
- Bonnie Moore, CEO, Moore Lead & Learn LLC
- Tiffany Prince, Founder and President, Prince Performance
- Laura Renaud, CPLP, Learning Leader, Medtronic
- Jennifer Rogers, CPLP, Chief Discovery Advocate, Development Ocean
- Lorinda Schrammel, Director, Talent Development, Oklahoma State University
- Katie Vaillancourt, Corporate Training Manager, Vaillancourt Corporate Training
- Linda Warren, CPLP, Director, Learning, Thornton Tomasetti

ATD Certification Institute Board of Directors
- Cynthia Allen, President, SeaCrest Consulting Company
- Michael Decker, Vice President, Examinations, AICPA
- Sean Walters, CEO and Executive Director, Investment & Wealth Institute
- Shannon Carter, Former Vice President, Education, SCRUM Alliance
- Dale Cyr, CEO and Executive Director, Inteleos

ATD Capability Model Project Team
- Holly Batts, Associate Director, Credentialing, ATD
- Kristen Fyfe-Mills, Director, Marketing and Strategic Communications, ATD
- Pat Galagan, Executive Editor, ATD
- Morgean Hirt, Director, Credentialing, ATD
- Jennifer Homer, Vice President, Community and Branding, ATD
- Courtney Vital, CPLP, Associate Vice President, Education, ATD

ATD Staff
- Elizabeth Decker, Senior Manager, Product Development
- Brandon Grubesky, Director, Membership
- Maria Ho, Associate Director, Research
- Tim Ito, Vice President, Content
- Paula Ketter, Content Strategist
- Amanda Miller, Senior Director, Enterprise Solutions
- Ann Parker, Senior Manager, Senior Leaders and Executives
- Nelson Santiago, Facilitator
- Jeff Surprenant, Senior Manager, Product Management and Learning Technologies
- Wei Wang, CPLP, Senior Director, Global

Editorial Support
- Carrie Cross, Cross Learning Consulting
- Jack Harlow, Developmental Editor, ATD Press
- Melissa Jones, Manager, ATD Press
- Mark Morrow, Independent Editorial Consultant
- Hannah Sternberg, Production Editor, ATD Press

References

Arneson, J., W.J. Rothwell, and J. Naughton. 2013. *ASTD Competency Study: The Training & Development Profession Redefined*. Alexandria, VA: ASTD Press.

Association for Talent Development (ATD). 2018a. *2018 State of the Industry*. Alexandria, VA: ATD Press.

Association for Talent Development (ATD). 2018b. *Lifelong Learning: The Path to Personal and Organizational Performance*. Alexandria, VA: ATD Press.

Association for Talent Development (ATD). 2019. *2019 Talent Development Salary and Benefits Report*. Alexandria, VA: ATD Press.

ATD Public Policy Council. 2018. *Bridging the Skills Gap*. Whitepaper. Alexandria, VA: Association for Talent Development.

Bernthal, P.R., K. Colteryahn, P. Davis, J. Naughton, W.J. Rothwell, and R. Wellins. 2004. *Mapping the Future: New Workplace Learning and Performance Competencies*. Alexandria, VA: ASTD Press.

Campion, M.A., A.A. Fink, B.J. Ruggeberg, L. Carr, G.M. Phillips, and R.B. Odman. 2011. "Doing Competencies Well: Best Practices in Competency Modeling." *Personnel Psychology* 64:225–262.

Collins, B. 2018. "Develop Your Career With Professional Certification." *TD at Work*. Alexandria, VA: ATD Press.

Eubanks, B. 2019. "Meeting Tomorrow's Skills Demands Today." *TD at Work*. Alexandria, VA: ATD Press.

Lasse, C. 2015. "How Can My Company Use Competency Models." ATD Insight, December 2. www.td.org/insights/how-can-my-company-use-competency-models.

McLagan, P.A., and D. Bedrick. 1983. *Models for Excellence*. Alexandria, VA: ASTD Press.

McLagan, P.A., and D. Suhadolnik. 1989. *Models for HRD Practice*. Alexandria, VA: ASTD Press.

Nagarajan, R., and R. Prabhu. 2015. "Competence and Capability—A New Look." *International Journal of Management* 6(6): 7–11.

Pinto, P., and J. Walker. 1978. *A Study of Professional Training and Development Roles and Competencies.* Alexandria, VA: ASTD Press.

Piskurich, G.M., and E.S. Sanders. 1998. *ASTD Models for Learning Technologies.* Alexandria, VA: ASTD Press.

Rothwell, W.J. 1996. ASTD *Models for Human Performance Improvement.* Alexandria, VA: ASTD Press.

Rothwell, W.J, and J. Graber. 2010. *Competency-Based Training Basics.* Alexandria, VA: ASTD Press.

Rothwell, W.J., E.S. Sanders, and J.G. Soper. 1999. *ASTD Models for Workplace Learning and Performance.* Alexandria, VA: ASTD Press.

Spencer, L.M., and S.M. Spencer. 1993. *Competence at Work: Models for Superior Performance.* New York: John Wiley & Sons.

About the Authors

Courtney Vital is a senior executive at the Association for Talent Development leading learning initiatives that enable professionals to achieve their potential, demonstrate their credibility, and advance their career. She is passionate about helping organizations reimagine how learning is designed and delivered to align with the realities of the modern workforce. With experience leading global learning businesses in the association, nonprofit, and for-profit environments, Courtney's areas of expertise include learning and education product strategy; program design and development, including learning ecosystems, credentialing, certificate and certification programs, workshops, events, and e-learning courses; evolving traditional learning products into modularized, digital learning experiences; assessment and evaluation; competency models and stackable learning and credentialing paths; and learning technology implementations.

Courtney has spent more than a decade at ATD, growing ATD's education business into a global training operation that has served more than 100,000 learners to date. She previously served as chief learning officer for the Human Capital Institute, where she oversaw HCI's strategy and thought leadership around learning, as well as a product line of certification programs targeted to senior HR professionals. She has a mix of subject matter expertise in the L&D, talent, and HR spaces, a deep technical understanding of learning experience design and development, and hands-on operational experience building education businesses. Courtney holds the Certified Professional in Learning and Performance credential, as well as a BA in journalism and mass communications from the University of North Carolina at Chapel Hill. She is a master's in adult education candidate at Pennsylvania State University. Courtney lives in the Washington, D.C., area with her husband and two daughters.

Patricia Galagan covered the training and talent development for nearly 40 years as a writer and editor for the Association for Talent Development (formerly ASTD) before retiring in 2019. She began her career as editor of ASTD's *Training & Development Journal* and was the founding editor of *Technical Training* magazine and *Learning Circuits*, ASTD's first digital magazine. With ATD CEO Tony Bingham, Pat interviewed more than 50 CEOs of major companies for the *TD* magazine series At C Level. She also wrote a quarterly column on trends in talent development for *TD* magazine for several years, and managed content for the Senior Leaders and Executives Community of Practice. Pat served as co-editor for *The Executive Guide to Integrated Talent Management* with Kevin Oakes.

Pat has an undergraduate degree in French from the College of St. Elizabeth, and a graduate degree in English from George Mason University. Since her retirement from ATD, Pat has turned her lifelong passion for photography into a full-time profession as a fine-art photographer based in Santa Fe, New Mexico. She and her husband, Philip Metcalf, co-authored *Fire Ghosts,* a photography book about new forest landscapes in an age of wildfires (George F. Thompson Publishing, 2019). Her photography has been shown at galleries in the United States, Cuba, and Switzerland.

As director of credentialing for the Association for Talent Development, **Morgean Hirt** brings more than 25 years of nonprofit experience in personnel certification and accreditation across a variety of professions. Morgean has devoted her career to advancing professions through the establishment of industry standards. She provides strategic leadership and technical expertise in developing and implementing credentialing programs, focusing on policy and standards development, test development, board and committee governance, program audits, strategic planning, and ANSI/ISO 17024 and NCCA accreditation.

Morgean has led a number of organizations through establishing industry standards for emerging professions, including clinical research, massage therapy, and mortgage brokering. Prior to joining ATD, Morgean spent 10 years as present and CEO of Certified Fund Raising Executives International Credentialing Board, and was responsible for establishing international support across six continents for a unified standard of fundraising practice. She also has served as a senior account executive with Metacred, a boutique association management firm specializing in credentialing management, where her clients included several IT-related associations. Morgean lives in the Washington, D.C., area and is an active member of the Institute for Credentialing Excellence (ICE), serving as a member of the Education and Program Committees and as a presenter at the ICE Exchange.